# ANNA AND DR HELMY

RONEN STEINKE

# ANNA AND DR HELMY

How an Arab Doctor Saved a
Jewish Girl in Hitler's Berlin

*Translated by*

SHARON HOWE

OXFORD
UNIVERSITY PRESS

# OXFORD
UNIVERSITY PRESS

Great Clarendon Street, Oxford, OX2 6DP,
United Kingdom

Oxford University Press is a department of the University of Oxford.
It furthers the University's objective of excellence in research, scholarship,
and education by publishing worldwide. Oxford is a registered trade mark of
Oxford University Press in the UK and in certain other countries

© Piper Verlag GmbH, München/Berlin 2017

The moral rights of the author have been asserted

First Edition published in 2021

Impression: 1

Published in the United States of America by Oxford University Press
198 Madison Avenue, New York, NY 10016, United States of America

British Library Cataloguing in Publication Data
Data available

Library of Congress Control Number: 2021943229

ISBN 978-0-19-289336-9

Printed and bound in Great Britain by
Clays Ltd, Elcograf S.p.A.

*For Hannah*

# ACKNOWLEDGEMENTS

Two of Anna's children—Carla Gutman Greenspan and Charles Gutman—received me in New York, spent days sharing family memories with me, and showed me an imitation crocodile leather suitcase that had lain in the attic for decades. Inside were letters, photos, and diaries in Yiddish, Hungarian, and German.

One nephew, two great-nephews, and the widow of another great-nephew of Dr Helmy's received me in Cairo, showed me their treasured photographs and entrusted me with Helmy's personal papers. They were Mohamed el-Kelish, Ahmed Nur el-Din Farghal, Prof. Dr med. Nasser Kotby, and Mervat el-Kashab.

My thanks to them all for their trust, openness, and warmth.

For advice, inspiration, and support, I thank Dr Sonja Hegasy, Yasser Mehanna and Teresa Schlögl from the Centre for Modern Oriental Studies (Berlin), Martina Voigt from the German Resistance Memorial Centre, Gili Diamant and Dr Irena Steinfeldt from Yad Vashem, Dr Irene Messinger (Vienna), Prof. Dr Peter Wien (Maryland), Prof. Dr David Motadel (LSE), Dr Jani Pietsch, Dieter Szturmann, Elisabeth Weber, Sabine Mülder, and Dr med. Karsten Mülder—to whom credit is due for uncovering Helmy's story in the first place, Amgad Youssef (Cairo), Sharon Howe for her superb translation of this book into English, and, last but not least, Ulrike, my first reader.

# CONTENTS

# CONTENTS

# MIDDLE EASTERN BERLIN

When the Gestapo barged into an Egyptian doctor's practice in Berlin in autumn 1943, they found a young Muslim woman sorting blood and urine samples behind the reception desk. She was fair-skinned, with a round face and intelligent eyes. Her dark hair was tied back beneath a sheer headscarf. When she smiled, her cheeks dimpled. And she smiled a lot—even during these encounters with the Gestapo.

People remembered her as tall and pretty. Full of energy—a picture of health, some said.[1] Others found her hard to describe. Oriental. Mediterranean. Wore a headscarf. What else was there to say about Dr Mohamed Helmy's Muslim assistant? A well assimilated young woman, certainly, one person commented. Few would have guessed at the time just how apt this compliment was.

The Gestapo officers barked their orders, demanding to see the boss—at once! Of course, the young woman assured them, the doctor would be with them presently. Would the gentlemen like to take a seat in the meantime?

Like Dr Helmy, she spoke with no trace of an accent, and her Arabic name, Nadia, was easy for Germans to pronounce. When asked where she came from, she explained that she was a relative of the doctor: his niece.

The Gestapo officers rummaged through drawers and flung open cabinet doors. They burst into the waiting room, suspiciously pulling back curtains, and no doubt ordering some of the patients to show their papers. Standing back at a discreet distance of a few metres, yet visible to all, Nadia dutifully assisted the officers.

Trains had been rolling into the extermination camps for two years now. It had begun with a march of shame through Berlin, on a bitingly cold day in autumn. On 18 October 1941, hundreds of Jewish men had been herded through the districts of Moabit, Charlottenburg, and Halensee. They had traipsed in the pouring rain though streets, across market squares, and down the Kurfürstendamm on their way to Grunewald station.

Now the Gestapo were hunting down those who had escaped the round-up. Thousands of Jews had gone to ground in Berlin. Many were homeless, sleeping under bridges or in woods. Others spent their days riding the U-Bahn, hiding in waiting rooms and toilets after the trains stopped running at night.

This wasn't the first time the Gestapo had shown up at the practice demanding to speak to the Muslim doctor. Nor was it the first time they had come asking about the whereabouts of one particular Jewish girl who had vanished. A girl named Anna.

Dr Helmy will be happy to help you however he can, the veiled assistant said. Just then, creaking floorboards announced that the doctor was about to take the Gestapo off her hands. A dark, gangling Egyptian came out of his surgery and approached the officers with his hand outstretched.

Heil Hitler, gentlemen.

'Some ladies keep miniature bulldogs. Some ladies wear monocles. Some ladies frequent gambling dens. And some ladies take up exotic religions.' Thus wrote 'Rumpelstiltskin'—otherwise known as Adolf Stein, a well-known national columnist for the *Berliner Lokalanzeiger*—in 1928. Berliners had tired of the Buddhists who came to worship at their temple in the wealthy suburb of Frohnau, he observed, and Krishnamurti was no longer in vogue among the capital's bohemians. 'Right now', he concluded, 'the most modern and fashionable thing in West Berlin is Islam.'[2]

In fact, a fascination with the Middle East had been evident in Berlin since at least the late nineteenth century. 'The Orient lives and breathes here,' the famous theatre critic Alfred Kerr wrote in his account of the Colonial Exhibition in Berlin in the summer of 1896. 'Bedouins, dervishes, Cairenes, Turks, Greeks, and their womenfolk are all present in undeniably authentic condition'.[3] The scent of Middle Eastern cardamom coffee mingled with the smell of two-pfennig Berlin cigarettes. Rumpelstiltskin, too, reported on the 'Mussulmen in gold-embroidered silk' who stood smoking outside their mud hut. But, he lamented, 'the large troupe we have been observing in the Zoological Garden this summer is of course no longer quite so primitive'. The human beings on show, he complained, had by now received 'a considerable lick of civilization'.[4] Berliners were completely captivated by the Orient, but they preferred to observe its people through the bars of a cage.

Arabs were exhibited in Berlin like exotic animals. In 1896, they had been put on show as part of a 'Tunisian Harem'; in 1927, they formed part of a 'Tripoli Exhibition'. Cairo and Palestine were other popular themes for human zoos. Cries of 'Excuse me!' and 'Stop pushing!' could be heard amid the jostling crowd of Berliners, as one journalist noted.[5] But a correspondent for the Jewish-German weekly *Allgemeine Zeitung des Judenthums* grew somewhat wistful at the sight of the miniature Cairo. The 'Oriental scene', he wrote, 'brings to mind so many biblical images', recalling 'the glorious past and sad present of my own people'.[6]

Jews and Muslims enjoyed a close relationship in Berlin, especially during the turbulent 1920s and 1930s, when the two groups discovered common ground and got along well with one another. Historians have long known that such a closeness existed. But the lengths to which it could go is a story hitherto untold.

Thanks to recent discoveries in the State Archive of Berlin and the Political Archive of the German Foreign Office, it has now come to light how Jews were hidden by Arabs to save them from the Nazis, in the very capital of Hitler's Reich. This is a story of hope in these times of hatred.

A perception shared by many Muslims in Western countries today is that the Holocaust had nothing to do with them, that it has no bearing on their own narrative, that Muslim migrants played no role in that dark phase of European history. This book is evidence to the contrary. The story of Mohamed Helmy and Anna Boros exemplifies the positive impact some Muslim immigrants had on Jewish lives amid the horror of the Holocaust. Drawing on historical documents, compensation claims, Gestapo correspondence, diplomatic papers, the personal records of the two protagonists and many hours of interviews with their surviving relatives, it shines a light on an all but forgotten world, the old Arabic Berlin of the Weimar period. This world was cultured, progressive, and, for the most part, anything but anti-Semitic.

A perception shared by many Jews in Western countries today is that the anti-Jewish sentiment rampant within some Muslim immigrant communities poses a grave threat. The historical events recounted in this book are not intended to provide solutions or comfort in the face of these present-day concerns. But the story of Helmy and Anna might at least offer hope that change is possible. The history of Muslims in Europe is older and more complex than it often seems today.

I do not wish to sugar-coat. Among the Muslims living in Berlin in the 1930s, there were some who assisted the Nazis and served the regime, helping to promote its anti-Semitic policies and propaganda or translating *Mein Kampf* into Arabic. But a considerable number of them also played a special role in resisting the persecution of Jews in Germany. This book is about those people, their achievements, and their courage.

# THE HOME VISIT

It must have been one afternoon in 1936 when Dr Mohamed Helmy and the young Anna first met. The girl had been deeply embarrassed by the grown-ups' behaviour that day; it was a spectacle she would remember long afterwards.

The streets of Berlin's Moabit district had been busy as Dr Helmy drove into the city centre, and he had had to keep stopping on his way to the Alexanderplatz, with its array of shop windows and advertising hoardings. In the Neue Friedrichstraße, he pulled up outside their smart town house, got out, and rang the bell. The ground floor of number 77 was almost completely occupied by a greengrocer's, and the scent of fruit wafted across the pavement towards him: fresh peaches from Italy, four marks a kilo, and fresh tomatoes, twenty pfennigs a kilo. He had been called here by a lady unknown to him.

The two women who greeted him at the front door had put on their finery for the occasion: diamond rings and necklaces. He had barely had chance to say hello before they began fussing round him, showering him with compliments. The housekeeper was summoned and dispatched to bring the doctor a cup of tea, the Hungarian cook to prepare a bite to eat. The doctor would no doubt be wanting a little refreshment? And the doctor needn't worry: it went without saying that no pork was served in their house.

Anna was just eleven years old at the time, and lived here with the two women—her mother Julie and her grandmother Cecilie. Listening to her mother fawning over the Egyptian stranger, she could hardly believe her ears. And now both of them were plying him with invitations in an attempt—as Anna described it—'to win over the doctor in a private capacity'.

Anna was 'not the sort to talk about her problems', as she later remarked. When something troubled her, she couldn't confide in either of her relatives, who appeared to her austere and ungenerous. They were hard women—perhaps because they had to be. The men in their family had left a legacy of inconstancy, premature death, and divorce, and so it was the women who ran the business. They were sparing with compliments and courtesies, which made this display for Dr Helmy's benefit all the more perplexing to the child. From where she stood, the women seemed to be 'throwing themselves' at their visitor.

Again and again they called her over, even though the doctor's visit had nothing to do with her. It was Anni here, Panny there. 'Pannyka!' her grandmother exclaimed in her Hungarian nagymama voice that always sounded equally sweet whether she was being kind or spiteful, *ne álljit a doktorúrútjába, teddmagadhasznossá!*—'Don't just stand there in the doctor's way—make yourself useful!'

Dr Helmy, who was just taking off his coat, hadn't dreamt of complaining that anyone was in his way. But Anna knew enough not to make a scene in front of her grandmother. 'I was fully aware of our situation,' she later recalled. Things had begun to go very badly for Jews, with 'the expropriation of shops, the seizure of money, and so on'. And so she held her tongue.

Just then the housekeeper brought the tea things, winding her way past the piano and the brocade-covered sofa, through a lounge containing a chaise-longue, two beds, two cupboards, and three rugs, and finally past paintings, china, and sculptures to the room where Anna's nagymama had chosen to be examined by the Arab doctor. This room—the parlour—boasted a glass cabinet, six armchairs, and the wall mirror that Cecilie called a 'trumeau'.

These were moneyed people, as Dr Helmy was meant to notice from the reflection in the trumeau. Perhaps that was why the women had called him out rather than coming in to the clinic. Downstairs in the greengrocery, M. Rudnik GmbH—named after Moise 'Max' Rudnik, Cecilie's second husband—the two women presided over tons of grapefruit and truckloads of pineapples. Over personnel, too. And over an annual turnover of hundreds of thousands of marks. Nevertheless, it cannot have escaped the doctor how nervous they were.

The firm handled a ton of grapes from Holland every month. With the introduction of the anti-Jewish laws, all that had become much more difficult; non-Jewish customers were lax about payment, causing problems for these and other Jewish tradespeople. Aubergines from Italy, figs from Greece, raisins from France, peppers, cucumbers, corn cobs, and pears from Hungary: nowadays all the import routes that had once made the business great were subject to restrictions. The Brandenburg turnip had never had it so good.

In the Central Market Hall, just a few yards down the Neue Friedrichstraße, signs had gone up saying 'No access to Jews until after noon.' In other words, not until all that was left were squashed tomatoes and half-rotten lettuces. Once, when Anna's mother Julie did her rounds at twenty to nine in the morning in defiance of the ban, she was reported by one of the traders and had a twenty-five-mark fine slapped on her by the police. But at least imports from the family's homeland still functioned, so that walnuts from the Black Sea continued to find their way into their Berlin shop window.

Was there anything else they could do for the doctor, and did he know that they imported from Arab countries too? Julie chattered incessantly, as was her wont when ill at ease. She had always had to fight for recognition. Her parents had once had high hopes for her, sending her to the Conservatoire for piano lessons. But there was no doubting what they thought of the popular pieces she

**Fig. 1.** The eleven-year-old Anna with her mother and stepfather, 1936

played at home, like Mischa Spoliansky's 'Morphine' or ragtime tunes with saucy lyrics.

Most Jewish doctors in Berlin had already lost their licences the previous year, in 1935, and things were even harder now for Jewish patients. As a Muslim, Dr Helmy enjoyed a privileged position: he was the only remaining 'non-Aryan' clinician in Berlin; what's more, he worked at one of the city's biggest hospitals, the Robert Koch Hospital in Moabit. It was an enviable post, as it also made him the only person who still had access to proper medication, such as strophantin for heart failure or real antibiotics like Salvarsan, as opposed to the dubious concoctions Jewish doctors had to make do with.

Consequently, Cecilie's affability towards her special guest was prompted more by desperation than genuine warmth. And she already sensed that Helmy must have another, darker side.

Later, she would hardly have a good word to say about him: not a word of thanks. Even after the war, she would write of him in a letter: 'Once a swine, always a swine.'

Overwhelming kindness was not a trait to which Cecilie was naturally inclined, as Anna knew, which made her effusiveness that afternoon all the more disconcerting. Anna's mother had not come to Berlin entirely of her own volition. Back home, she had lived together with the Jewish factory owner Ladislaus Boros. After their marriage, their new-born child Anna had been a gift from heaven. But by then Cecilie had already gone ahead to Berlin and wanted her daughter to follow her there. So she hired a private detective in order to prove Ladislaus Boros guilty of philandering. The detective did his job, the marriage broke up, and Julie got divorced. Left to cope alone with the two-year-old Anna, she made her way with a heavy heart to Berlin. Just as Cecilie had planned.

Now, sitting before the trumeau with the Muslim doctor, she was all sweetness and light. Anna cringed inwardly. The Hungarian cook came in and set down the tray with refreshments. Please, be our guest, doctor! the two women purred, and Anna wouldn't have been surprised if her mother had got up and sat at the piano to impress the new guest, as she so often did. Franz Behr's 'Cajolery' would have been perfect for the occasion, Anna later bitterly reflected.

# A SCENT OF TEA

Anna's grandmother still clearly remembered the day—1 April 1933—when Nazi Stormtroopers first came and stood outside their greengrocer's store on the Alexanderplatz, shouting anti-Jewish slogans and urging people to boycott their business. The few token figures had made rather a pathetic spectacle in the drizzling rain and soon went away again, much to the family's relief.[1] The real dogs of war had been unleashed elsewhere that day: at Moabit hospital, where several SA Storm 33 trucks had driven right up between the red-brick wings of the building. It was the hospital where the Egyptian Dr Helmy happened to work.

'Storm 33'—known as the 'Murder Storm'—were the most hardened thugs among the Brownshirts. Two dozen of them had jumped out of their trucks and swarmed over the place. Brandishing pre-prepared lists, they had marched to each ward and removed Jewish doctors from consulting rooms and operating theatres.

'Will you just allow me to hand over my patients to my senior physician?' the director of the neurological department, Professor Kurt Goldstein, had asked when the SA turned up at his door, but they only shouted back in his face: 'Everyone is replaceable–including you!'[2]

The Jewish doctors were all still in their white coats as the SA herded them onto the waiting trucks in the courtyard. They were taken to the former barracks on General-Pape-Straße, where the Brownshirts had set up their headquarters. Exulting in their recent elevation to the status of 'auxiliary police', the SA officers registered and logged everything in meticulous detail. Each prisoner was given a docket on which their name and occupation were neatly entered, as if all this were regulation procedure. Reflecting on this episode, the writer Lion Feuchtwanger later remarked that the 'military bureaucracy' with which the abuses in the Pape-Straße were organized was almost the most chilling aspect of all.[3] That night, an orgy of violence began in the basement. Some of the doctors were brutally murdered, beaten to death with truncheons.[4]

The next day, the hospital lay silent, as if deserted. The vast majority of its doctors—a good two thirds—had been Jewish, and now they were gone. That had been the distinguishing feature of this hospital, built between the potholes and moonshine distilleries of Moabit, amid that mix of brick housing, advertising pillars, fire escapes, and washing lines so characteristic of poorer quarters the world over. As one doctor recalled, the place had been 'inundated' with Moabit's casualties ever since the Great Depression of 1929.[5]

It was this that made Anna's grandmother so mistrustful of Dr Helmy's character from the moment she heard about him. An Egyptian still working at the hospital three years after the Brownshirt raid? She only had to put two and two together.

That barked instruction of the SA in 1933—'Everyone is replaceable!—hadn't, it seemed, applied to Helmy. Clearly, he was in the opposite camp: one of those ready to step into the victims' shoes.

An Arab of all people! Cecilie must have thought. How close the bond had been between the small group of Arabs in Berlin and the much larger group of Jews; how much Arabs in this city owed to Jews! Thousands of young men from Arab countries had come to Berlin, the city's universities attracting the sons of the best Cairene or Damascene families.

When Helmy arrived here in October 1922 to study medicine,[6] it would have been hard to imagine a more bizarre place. The Germans had just assassinated their Foreign Minister, Walther Rathenau, the first Jew to occupy the post. A mood of nervousness pervaded the city that could tip over into aggression at any moment. The stock exchange had fallen into a deep hole and the place was on its knees. Women in headscarves and aprons pushed wheelbarrows full of banknotes through the streets. 'Like mille-feuille pastry', one foreign visitor observed, 'a one-mark note multiplied under the influence of a mysterious force that changed it into a thousand-note wad. The duplicating machinery of the sorcerers' apprentices at the Berlin Mint whirred incessantly.'[7] It wasn't bad news for everyone, however: 'You can live well on ten pounds a month', an Egyptian medical student enthused in a Cairo newspaper after living in Berlin for a while.[8] For Egyptians, the exchange rates were a dream come true. Especially those from well-to-do backgrounds like Helmy, the son of an Egyptian army major.

When Helmy's nephews came over from Egypt to visit him, he took them as a matter of course to the city's cultural icons, such as the bust of the Egyptian queen Nefertiti on Museum Island, a place of pilgrimage since 1924. But he also made time for the worldlier pleasures of its gourmet temples. Roast pork, ham, wine: nothing was taboo. 'Go on, try it, habibi!' he teased them. 'It's good for you. Trust me—I'm a doctor.'[9]

The Arab guest students were welcomed with open arms in this city. After winding their way northwards from the southern tip of Italy on smooth-rolling, brass-trimmed sleeper trains, they would arrive at the city's Anhalter Bahnhof station to find German women waiting for them on the platform, dressed in their Sunday best. The Middle Eastern guests took rooms in middle-class homes, their rent providing a lifeline for many a family. The majority were concentrated around the Kurfürstendamm, the city's chic shopping boulevard, from where they enjoyed a view over cabaret clubs, coffee houses, and the stump-shaped caps of the Prussian police. For some of the Arab students, it was almost like being adopted, and Helmy too was invited at weekends to play tennis or go hiking or sailing.[10] More often than not, it was Jewish families who extended the hand of friendship. Sometimes out of fellow feeling, sometimes sheer romanticism.

These were the days when the Jewish poet Else Lasker-Schüler could be seen promenading along the Kurfürstendamm dressed as Yusuf, the flute-playing Arabian prince whose persona she adopted in her writings. In *Hebräerland* ('Land of the Hebrews'), a romanticized account of Palestine written after her first visit there, she expresses a longing for reconciliation between the Jewish and Arab peoples, who are characterized as stepbrothers named Joseph and Yusuf.

A fellow orientalist poet of the day was Lev Nussimbaum, whose books were the talk of Berlin's salons and bars. Born in Baku, Azerbaijan, the son of a Jewish oil trader, he subsequently changed his name to Muhammad Essad Bey, and would turn up for his readings at the Café des Westens in turban, harem pants, and earrings.

When the imam and his assistant first arrived in Berlin in 1925, they sub-rented from a Jewish family, the Oettingers, on the

Kurfürstendamm.[11] There was a long tradition of interest in Arab culture among Jewish scholars: in the nineteenth century, the liberal rabbi Abraham Geiger had studied Arabic and the Quran,[12] and the open evenings of the Berlin mosque were now attended by so many Jewish guests that Gestapo informers visiting in 1934 reported that the Muslim house of prayer was providing 'a lair and flophouse for Kurfürstendamm Jews.'[13] What's more, the openness of this community was such that, 'at their gatherings, when the participants believe they are among comrades, they [have] apparently made derogatory comments about National Socialism and its Führer'.[14]

The mosque, with its twin 32-metre-tall minarets, stylized crenellations, and lanterns, stood in the Fehrbelliner Platz in the city's Wilmersdorf district. Built in 1925, it was like a miniature Taj Mahal: an architectural tribute to the Indian Mogul masterpiece in Agra. The project was the work of missionaries from Lahore in British India—colleagues of Gottlieb Wilhelm Leitner, a Hungarian Jew who lectured in Arabic and Islamic sharia law at King's College London.[15]

The outside of the building was white, the inside a riot of Asiatic colour: ochre, red, and aquamarine—not exactly to the plain geometric taste of Egyptian Sunnis like Helmy. To one eager neophyte, however—a First World War veteran decorated with the Iron Cross—it was a 'dream in marble, a poem in stone'.[16] Chalid-Albert Seiler-Chan, a German soldier who had converted to Islam after returning from the front, was among those who could still remember the days when the first Muslims in Berlin had to conduct their prayer services on the roof of the Treptow Observatory.[17]

Normally, visitors to the mosque were charged thirty pfennigs,[18] but Berlin's Muslim community also held special evenings during the 1920s to which diplomats, literary figures, and scholars were personally invited.[19] Beneath the turquoise alcoves of the building, people sang songs; a man in a cashmere scarf recited the poetry of Iqbal, whom he introduced to the public as an Indian Rilke; four Tatars from the Urals performed a traditional folksong, and trays of tea, dates, and halva were passed around.[20]

Gazing up at the dome, one German newspaper reporter marvelled at how 'the subtle fire of bright Oriental rugs enhances the ceremonial beauty of the mosque's interior'. It was a Wednesday in February 1931, and the Muslim community was celebrating its principal religious holiday Eid al-fitr, the breaking of the fast at the end of Ramadan. By then, Helmy was already a junior doctor at the hospital—a strenuous job, from which moments like this offered some respite.

Elsewhere in Berlin, the whiff of gunpowder hung in the air. In the parliament building, a couple of Social Democrats had been thrown from the public gallery by Communists. The city council meeting had descended into a loud slanging match, and the tumult had ended with a twenty-two-year-old Nazi firing eight shots into the crowd with a revolver.[21] At the mosque, by contrast, the mood was one of calm contemplation. 'We sit at the Muslims' tea table', the visiting German reporter rhapsodized, 'and the spicy aroma of the dark infusion mingles with the subtle perfume of the flowers before us.'[22]

By rights, Helmy should have returned to Cairo in 1931. Having funded his medical studies, his family expected him to come home and support them now that he had his degree from Berlin's Friedrich-Wilhelm University in the bag.[23] But he was far too happy in the German capital.

**Fig. 2.** In the garden of the Berlin mosque—a meeting place for scholars and literary figures

Walther Rathenau had once described his native city on the river Spree as 'the parvenu of cities, and the city of parvenus'. He saw 'nothing to be ashamed of' in this, however: a parvenu was, after all, nothing more than a self-made man.[24] And that was exactly how the young Dr Helmy felt about his own life. In Cairo, he would have had to start all over again. His Arabic had grown rusty, and he had already begun to trip over the words, or they escaped him, as was evident from his letters. So he resisted the calls of his family and stayed in the place that had long since become home. This led to something of a rupture, particularly with his eldest brother in Cairo—an officer who had grown into the role of head of the family.[25]

One of the world's most eminent authorities in Helmy's field of internal medicine was the elegant, white-moustachioed Jewish professor Georg Klemperer, son of a liberal rabbi from Brandenburg and brother of the writer Victor Klemperer. A senior consultant at Moabit hospital, he had declared himself impressed with the Egyptian guest student's 'great commitment'.[26] The professor was generally known for giving priority to Jewish applicants, no doubt out of a sense of solidarity. There was nowhere else for Jewish doctors to go, he said, and it was therefore his duty to take them.[27] But the same impulse had also prompted him to take the young Muslim—an outsider in the world of German clinics and institutes—under his wing.

'You see,' the professor once said to his staff, 'the difference between an Aryan doctor and a Jewish one is this: the Jewish doctor regards his work as a service—he is there to serve the patient—whereas the Aryan doctor is a commander, giving orders.'[28] Of these two stereotypes, Klemperer had evidently placed the talented young Helmy in the former category. He entrusted increasingly important tasks to his protégé, who 'applied himself with particular zeal to the pathology of the urogenital system',[29] and wrote appreciatively that Helmy had 'adapted extremely well to the German language and customs and to the mentality of our people—and was never regarded by the patients as a foreigner'.[30]

Helmy was not the only Arab medical student to be given such an opportunity: others included Mohamed el-Hadari, who trained at the neighbouring gynaecology clinic under Dr Max Hirsch,[31] or the Syrian Wassil Rasslan, who soon also became the leader of Berlin's Islamic community. Helmy's boss, Professor Klemperer, corresponded with institutes from Madrid to Moscow, and experimented in the field of psychosomatics and placebo effects, which were entirely new at the time. On one occasion, at a carnival ball in the doctors' mess, he submitted to some affectionate teasing on this score from his small group of Jewish and Muslim trainees, one of whom had penned a song caricaturing him as a hypnotist and satirizing the technique of suggestion. Accompanying it on the piano was the senior physician of the department, Dr Max Leffkowitz, a small man with round spectacles and unruly hair who became involved with the radically left-wing Association of Socialist Doctors, along with another Jewish doctor, Alfred Döblin, nowadays remembered less for his medical skills than as the author of the famous novel *Berlin Alexanderplatz*.[32]

In those days, it had been rare for any member of staff at Dr Helmy's hospital to express sympathy for Hitlerism—and they were given short shrift if they did. In one encounter with a Nazi doctor, a colleague of Helmy's remarked, 'You're so far up the Führer's arse you'd come out the other side if there wasn't an ileocecal valve in the way!'[33] By this, he meant the sphincter muscle between the large and small intestine—a part of the body with which Helmy, as a trainee in the Department of Internal Medicine I,[34] was intimately acquainted.

After the brutal beatings of 1 April 1933, all that changed. In the hospital basement where they imprisoned their victims, the SA thugs had made senior consultant Leffkowitz crawl on all fours, bark like a dog and shout 'Heil Hitler!', before forcing him up against the wall and firing shots around his silhouette like a knife-thrower at a fairground.[35]

A few days later, Max Leffkowitz returned to the hospital one last time: to collect his references.[36] But the request elicited barely a shrug from one of the remaining non-Jewish members of staff: 'Leffkowitz was the biggest Jew of all.'[37]

Helmy was also at the hospital that day. His personnel file, too, lay on the table. Instead of being expelled like his many Jewish colleagues, however, he was promoted, at the age of just thirty-one, to the rank of senior consultant—the very post that Leffkowitz had previously occupied.

It must have been bewildering for Helmy to find himself treated so differently from the Jewish colleague who had supported him all those years, at a hospital where—according to its detractors—it was impossible to get on unless you were Jewish.[38] Yet he acquiesced in this sudden invitation to share in the spoils of the Nazi raid. He accepted one of the 'vacated' postdoctoral positions (as the SA described them) along with a grant from the Friedrich-Wilhelm University; nor did he protest when the new rulers ordered him to break off all relations with his old Jewish colleagues.[39] His long-time companions must have eyed him with disbelief. Helmy had been one of them. Yet now he was forging ahead without them, buoyed up on the same brown wave that bore them down. Did it feel like a betrayal to Helmy too?

There had been romances between Jews and Muslims, and mixed marriages had been celebrated in the mosque, notably that of the student Khwaja Abdul Hamid to his fiancée, Luba, in 1928.[40] And there were Jews who had converted to Islam, such as the young artist couple Leopold Weiss and Elsa Schiemann-Specht. Travelling on the Berlin U-Bahn after a sojourn in the Middle East, they had found themselves sitting in silence opposite a businessman clinging jealously to his briefcase. To them, he had seemed to embody the kind of mean, hard, shallow-minded mentality that had brought a politically volatile Europe to the verge of destruction in 1914 to 1918. It was at that moment, they later claimed, that they

decided to become Muhammad and Aziza Asad (meaning 'lion')—
two new members of the city's small but steadily growing Muslim
community.[41]

Even the manager of Berlin's mosque during the twenties and
thirties was a Jewish convert to Islam. Dr Hugo Marcus was a man
whose dark moustache lent him an air of severity at odds with the
childlike quality of his large round eyes. A writer from East
Prussia, Marcus had celebrated his first literary success at just
twenty-four. In this book, *Meditationen*, he had developed the idea
of a utopian renewal of Europe by lay priests belonging to a universal brotherhood.[42] Despite converting to Islam, he still remained
a member of Berlin's Jewish community.[43] Indeed, he saw no con-
tradiction between the two religions, arguing that they both
shared a clear monotheism, without the adjunct of a son of God,
or the power of an established Church. Adopting Islam had simply
allowed him to retain his existing world view while giving him
access to some of the ground-breaking thinkers of human history.[44]

Marcus, who had renamed himself Hamid, was also a politically active figure, campaigning for the abolition of the infamous
paragraph 175 of the German Criminal Code under which homosexual men were persecuted, and which the Nazis would later
tighten even more dramatically. He was a regular contributor to
the journal *Sexus* published by his friend, the sexologist Magnus
Hirschfeld, and wrote under the pen name Hans Alienus for the
homosexual magazine *Der Kreis*.[45] While visiting an art exhibition
with Hirschfeld, he had once showed his companion a portrait of
himself by the feminist Jewish painter Julie Wolfthorn.[46]

When the columnist 'Rumpelstiltskin' came to the mosque to
ask about the role of women in Islam, the imam Dr Abdullah
answered him in German that Islam was the first religion to grant

women the same rights as men. 'You must be joking!' Rumpelstiltskin retorted, 'if it hadn't been for Mustafa Kemal rolling back the power of Islam, women in Turkey wouldn't have the freedom they enjoy today.'[47] But Berlin's Muslims had a different understanding of their faith: one that was open-minded, cosmopolitan, and progressive.

The notion of Jewish–Muslim kinship was also invoked by Hugo 'Hamid' Marcus in the *Moslemische Revue,* in an article on the Jewish Enlightenment philosopher Baruch Spinoza, whom he described as being 'already connected with Islam through his ancestry'. Spinoza, he explained, came from the Dutch Jewish community—descendants of those Jews who had seen their happiest days under the rule of Islam in Spain, until they were driven out of the country. Spain's Moorish Muslims had willingly shared their intellectual heritage and advanced philosophical and scientific culture with their Jewish brothers. According to Marcus, it was therefore 'no wonder that the offspring of those Jews, exiled to Holland, still embodied the intellectual legacy that their forebears owed to Muslims'.[48]

As for Dr Leffkowitz, he left Germany for Palestine with his wife after the fateful beatings of 1933.[49] Professor Klemperer emigrated to the USA. When asked in later life about his sudden career leap that year, Helmy always prevaricated. 'Vacancies had become available'[50] was all he would say—whether out of shame or dishonesty.

In black-and-white photographs taken between 1933 and 1937, Helmy can be seen surrounded by the new Nazi medics who quickly moved in to fill the gaps left by the Jewish doctors. The men stand close together, some with a broad, defiant grin, arms folded. Of the many new faces, most were drawn from the ranks of the SA and SS. What had once been the city's most 'Jewish' hospital had turned almost overnight into a hotbed of Nazism. Some of those pictured bear duelling scars, such as the SS colonel Dr Heinrich Teitge, who had stepped into Professor Klemperer's shoes as senior physician in charge of the Department of Internal Medicine I. This made him a direct colleague of Helmy, who took over the same post in Department II. Just a couple of years later, Teitge would become 'Minister of Health' under Hans Frank in the General Government district of Poland, where he was responsible for 'sanitary facilities' in the extermination camps of Treblinka, Sobibor, and Majdanek.[51]

In the photograph, all the doctors are wearing the same white coats, but the hierarchy is clear. All are on their feet except for Dr Helmy, who sits gazing into the distance with a still, solemn air.[52] As one of the doctors of the time recalls, 'On ward rounds, the boss would appear like some kind of god with an entourage of younger assistants busy scribbling down his every word.'[53] An Arab leading the Nazi medical team: astonishing to think how long it lasted.

# 'OF RELATED BLOOD'

Under the new hospital regime, head nurses were in danger of losing their caps from so many Hitler salutes. The corridors echoed with the bluster of 'uniformed doctors dressed up in white coats and devoid of any technical expertise', as one of the sisters privately sneered.[1] The Egyptian in their midst later shuddered to recall the 'bizarre treatment methods' that the new staff introduced and which 'very often put patients in mortal danger'.[2]

Helmy was under no illusion: when the SA dragged his Jewish colleagues from their offices on 1 April 1933, they would have preferred to throw him out likewise. As a fellow 'non-Aryan', he too should have fallen foul of the 'personnel adjustment at this almost exclusively Jewish hospital', in the terminology of the Nazi personnel commissar.[3]

Most Nazis still had in mind the passage from *Mein Kampf* in which all Arabs were characterized as inferior, and their anti-colonial campaign against the French and British a 'coalition of cripples'. In it, Hitler had written: 'As a folkish man, who appraises the value of men on a racial basis, I am prevented by mere knowledge of the racial inferiority of these so-called "oppressed nations" from linking the destiny of my own people with theirs.'[4] Similar sentiments were expressed by the Nazi ideologue Alfred Rosenberg in his book *The Myth of the Twentieth Century*, in which he explicitly welcomed the subjugation of Arab nations to the will of Europe.

As it happened, Helmy had a German girlfriend—a practice nurse named Emmy Ernst. Whenever he walked out with her on his arm, the spectacle of this elegantly suited and hatted man and his considerably younger companion would invariably draw disapproving glances. Sometimes Arab students were attacked for courting German women. In one case in February 1934, a foreign student, Fuad Hasanayn Ali, was abused at a dance hall in Tübingen for being 'black, of inferior race and therefore unfit to dance with a German lady'.[5]

Helmy's girlfriend was a cheerful, open-minded sort, who radiated self-confidence with her expensive jewellery and tailored jackets. But at a time when girls who dated Jews were forced to parade shaven-headed through villages advertising their shame on a sign around their necks, she was also brave.

When the Nazi government introduced the Nuremberg Laws in 1935—the net it cast to catch its murder victims—Helmy was astonished at the extent to which Muslims were spared. Signs stipulating 'No persons of foreign race' outside swimming baths were soon refined to 'No Jews'[6] in response to the alarm expressed by Arab embassies in Berlin. When the Nazi judicial system set out to track down and prosecute those guilty of 'racial defilement', Helmy and Emmy were gripped with fear. But a similar thing happened again.

According to the Hitler government's legal commentators, the term 'of related blood' could only be applied to Europeans, with the possible exception of Turks, who had been an ally of Germany in the First World War. But what about Arabs like Helmy? Drawing on confidential sources within the German government, the magazine *Le Temps* ran a story on 14 June 1936 claiming that Hitler's bureaucrats no longer counted Near and Middle Eastern peoples as racially acceptable. Outraged, *La bourse égyptienne* translated this into a headline suggesting that Egyptians were classed alongside Jews in Germany.[7] But the Foreign Office immediately went into conciliatory mode. The racial laws, it assured them, were only aimed at Jews. Muslims had no reason to fear.

So, were Arabs 'related' or 'alien'? Logic dictated that the Nazi regime could only assign them to one side or the other; the Nuremberg Laws didn't allow for a third category. It was a situation that left government lawyers wrestling with their own racial ideology until they tied themselves in knots. Finally, at a meeting of all the relevant ministries at the Foreign Office on 1 July 1936, it was established that Arabs, if not actually genetically 'related', should nevertheless be placed on an 'equal footing' with Europeans.[8]

This measure ensured that Arabs like Helmy would not share the fate of the Jews. Consequently, Helmy didn't have to hide his relationship with Emmy, and could even move up the career ladder while all around him his Jewish colleagues were being maltreated and thrown out onto the street. The Nazi strategists were keen to incentivize Muslims like him to get on board with the regime, and the new hospital management was therefore compelled against its will to promote him all the way to the rank of senior physician and place him in charge of a ward.[9]

It was the strategists in the background, the ministerial architects of future wars, who kept their Brownshirt foot soldiers in check. This was the reason behind Helmy's surprising career leap in the spring of 1933: his appointment as a doctor at Moabit hospital was, as his supervisor declared in 1934, 'also highly desirable

**Fig. 3.** The 'mixed couple' attracted disapproving looks: Helmy with his German fiancée, Emmy, on the streets of Berlin

in the interests of Germans abroad, according to the statements of the Foreign Office and the (Egyptian) legation'.[10] However great the temptation to the contrary, the Stormtroopers were obliged to restrain themselves.

All this was part of a political calculation by the Nazi leadership to get the Muslim world on its side. The aim was to harness what the party ideologue Rosenberg had described as a 'violent intellectual mood...in the Islamic world...led by the fanatical spirit of Mohammed'. Now that the Nazi strategists were focusing on preparations for war and possible alliances on the fringes of Europe, Muslims appeared attractive partners against the rival nations of France and England. At the same time, Paris and London were themselves busy trying to cultivate the Middle East, and had suddenly begun funding the construction of mosques, for example.

All references to similarities between Islam and Judaism, such as dietary regulations or ritual circumcision—previously seized on with relish by papers such as *Der Stürmer*—were now considered undesirable. Hitler's propaganda minister, Goebbels, had warned the press to refrain from all slurs against Muslims: instead, Islam was to be praised as anti-Bolshevist and anti-Semitic.[11] Except that the Nazis soon dropped the term 'anti-Semitic' in order to avoid alienating Arabs, lest they should interpret 'Semitic' as referring to them also.

This expression had been borrowed from linguistics. Although Hebrew and its two siblings, Aramaic and Arabic, are Semitic languages, those who speak them are not 'Semites'. To be on the safe side, however, the regime confined itself to the term 'anti-Jewish' from 1935 onwards. Thus, the government department for 'anti-Semitic action' was renamed accordingly, and the newspapers were compelled on Goebbels's orders to strike the word 'anti-Semitism' from their vocabulary.

Sometimes, Emmy would tease her fiancé, Helmy, for being more German than most Germans, with his punctuality, precision, and seriousness, his dark suits and his Mercedes. He had even come to share Emmy's love of dogs.[12] It was she who advised him to use his childhood nickname Mohd instead of Mohamed: that way, Berliners wouldn't instantly think of the Quran and Mohammedans when addressing him.[13]

Although extremely common in the Arab world, the name Mohamed was problematic in Germany. To German ears, it had a ring of pathos about it, like that of Jesus. Thus, Mohamed became Mohd, and was shortened even further to Mod after the war. Helmy made a point of using his nickname wherever he could— on his doctoral thesis, on new ID cards and in letterheads—even though both the Egyptian and German authorities stuck rigidly to Mohamed in their records.

Perhaps Helmy even tried to go with the political flow in the early days, at least for a short time. A testimonial of 1934 indicates that his bosses at the hospital found him less objectionable than the numerous upstarts from the SA and SS. They saw in him a flexible opportunist. 'Although a foreigner, Dr Helmy's conduct demonstrated a consistently pro-German attitude,' they wrote. Indeed, 'as far as he could, he engaged sympathetically with all national endeavours'.[14]

# A FOOL'S LICENCE

Helmy would have liked to be a more sociable member of staff. But how could he, with these new colleagues? To his horror, patients suddenly began dying in their droves after routine operations such as the removal of an appendix or gall bladder. This was virtually unheard of.[1] As one of the junior doctors subsequently mocked, a large proportion of the new Nazi medical officers who certified patients as insane were themselves 'teetering on the edge of insanity'.[2]

The recruitment criteria for new medical staff in 1933 had been defined by the SA itself: 'Now that the walls of the Jewish liberalist-Marxist stronghold have been brought down by persistent pressure, it is important that we fill every office of our rebuilt nation with the pioneers responsible for this victory...it is altogether a common mistake to demand specialist expertise and experience from the Stormtrooper first and foremost...a demand that cannot usually be met...'[3]

The consequences of this policy were immediately apparent in the surgical department, whose new head was actually a sports physician. His chief accomplice, the senior surgical consultant Dr Kurt Strauss, was an SS major and, as one nurse later recalled, a 'complete waste of space'. According to her, Strauss was 'utterly incompetent as a surgeon'.[4] On one occasion, he accidentally

sewed the patient's gut to his abdominal wall, with fatal consequences.[5] In the case of another patient who had swallowed a
spoon, he opened the man's stomach under local anaesthetic,
causing him to cry out at every cut and every stitch. This time, the
patient was in such pain that Strauss didn't even try to sew the
abdominal wall back together, but made do with a dressing to
staunch the blood. The man in question was a political prisoner
who had been brought to the hospital from remand custody. The
next day, after poking around in the wound with a pair of twee-
zers, the SS surgeon gloated: 'There, we'll make a good German of
you yet.'[6]

The man was plainly a sadist. And Helmy wasn't afraid to say
so. He rebuked the young, inexperienced Nazi doctors when they
maltreated patients and, according to one increasingly irate Nazi
senior consultant, 'had no compunction about damaging the
reputation of German doctors in front of patients and nursing
staff'.[7] In different times, a hospital can be a refuge from the world
of politics—a place untouched by matters of ideology. In Helmy's
case, however, it was the very source of his politicization.

Any initial respect he may have felt for the Brownshirts was
soon in short supply. And if his sense of intellectual superiority
over the Nazis needed any confirmation, he found it now in
spades. The more the procedures at the hospital began to repel
him, the more clearly he remembered the old Jewish–Muslim solidarity that had flourished here until 1933.

Muslim Berlin had been a place of culture: the *Moslemische Revue*,
the journal of the mosque association, proudly noted that its
events had been attended by the likes of Albert Einstein, Martin
Buber, Martin Niemöller, Thomas Mann, and Hermann Hesse.[8]
'When I see a tiny insect land on my paper while I am engaged in

my calculations,' the former visitor Albert Einstein wrote in a letter of 1952, 'I feel something akin to the conviction that Allah is great and we are but feeble creatures for all our scientific glory'[9]— a remark that reveals, if not identification with the Muslim faith, then certainly empathy with and respect for it.

In those days, there was a shared nostalgia for the ancient Orient and the comparatively harmonious coexistence of religions there. 'In Baghdad, the works of Aristotle and Plato were read with a youthful thirst for knowledge', one contributor to the *Moslemische Revue* wrote enthusiastically of the historic Caliphate of Baghdad in the tenth century AD. 'Mathematics and astronomy followed in the footsteps of Euclid and Ptolemy, while the sick were treated courtesy of Hippocrates and Galen', the ancient Greek pioneer of the science of anatomy.[10] This appreciation was shared by Helmy's professors. In June 1929, they honoured the tradition of their Muslim guests by celebrating the thousandth birthday of the Arab doctor Abu'l-Kasim at Berlin's Charité hospital, with coffee specially donated by the proprietor of the major coffee-roasting house 'Mokka', Hamid Abu'l-Kasim.[11]

Back then, people met in the evening at cultural clubs, in societies and discussion groups, at readings, lectures, and concerts. One discussion group was more conservative, the other more liberal. One was vehemently anti-colonial, the other more circumspect. The groups vied with each other, producing endless critiques and a stream of publications. A good dozen Muslim magazines appeared in Berlin at the time, most of them in German.[12]

There were debates at the Oriental Club on Kalckreuthstraße and dances in the Islamic Institute premises at Fasanenstraße 23. This building had been a gift from the Kaiser himself to his Arab guests. With its herringbone parquet flooring and marble fireplace, it could almost have been taken for a classic European gentlemen's club, were it not for the pyramids, palms, and even camels which its over-zealous donor had had painted on the walls. Many decades later, it would be taken over by the Berlin Literaturhaus, which remains there to this day.

In Helmy's time, this was the venue for meetings of the student association Islamia. Founded in 1924, this organization also staged protests against the racist ethnological exhibitions which were still bringing in a tidy profit for zoos. As one newspaper commentator sighed: 'The people of Berlin have doubtless played their own substantial part in making the Oriental visitor lose the respect he has been brought up to feel for all Europeans.'[13]

When one of the Nazi doctors accused Helmy during an argument of being 'a guest with a poor command of the German language and incapable of writing documents in German',[14] he was talking utter nonsense: Helmy's letters were written in sophisticated German, and he spoke with barely a trace of an accent.[15] He had trained with professors of the highest renown during the Weimar years, having already attended the best schools in Egypt. All the men in his family were officers, and he had been accustomed to military manners longer than most of the SA doctors. He had sat his higher-level exams at the Saideya high school in Cairo's neighbouring city of Giza, within walls adorned with portraits of ministers and generals who had once studied there.[16]

In Berlin, Helmy's weekends were not spent in the 'beer temples and sausage palaces' as Walther Rathenau once mockingly described them[17], but amongst books and on the tennis courts of the Hohenzollerndamm, which were also frequented by the young imam of the Wilmersdorf mosque, Dr Muhammad Abdullah, and his Indian wife.[18]

**Fig. 4.** A Muslim among Nazis: Helmy and staff at Moabit hospital

The good reputation of Moabit hospital soon deteriorated under its new rulers. Things got so bad that ambulance drivers would advise patients to go anywhere but there for surgery. Even in Dr Helmy's own department of internal medicine, his colleagues were beginning to have qualms, and attempted to send their patients to other hospitals rather than to their own surgical department under the notorious Dr Strauss.[19] Indeed, the SS surgeon would soon have run out of work if it hadn't been for the Nazi genetic health courts, which referred Moabit's delinquents to him for sterilization.

Once, they sent him a sixteen-year-old girl from a children's home. The reason given in her file was simply that 'She was in the habit of gadding about with boys till late at night, visiting and dancing at fairgrounds, and dressing conspicuously...As she had not had a proper upbringing and was unable to grasp the immorality of her behaviour due to her mental insufficiency, she was living a life in which her urges were being allowed to go entirely unchecked.'[20] She too was among those whom Dr Strauss deprived of the opportunity of motherhood at the state's behest. Around four hundred female patients died at the hospital as a result of such operations in 1934 and 1935 alone.[21]

Helmy made no secret of his abhorrence. To avoid a clash with his dim-witted new boss, the NSDAP member Helmut Dennig, he arranged to be transferred from his department to the *Zinnsoldaten* ('tin soldiers'), as the medical staff working under Professor Wilhelm Zinn—an essentially liberal-minded senior consultant from Switzerland—were known.

Before long, however, Zinn too was replaced by another Party member, Werner Sieber, and Helmy faced the same problems again. In a letter, Sieber wrote disparagingly of the Egyptian: 'After an initially smooth cooperation, there were various complaints from the other doctors regarding his arrogance and dogmatic, uncomradely manner.'[22]

Thereafter, the Nazi chiefs tried their level best to get rid of Helmy. First, the senior consultant Dennig attested to his 'distinctly Oriental manners'—a phrase intended in anything but a complimentary sense. 'As an Oriental, Dr H. was unable to adapt to the order, discipline, and professional ethos of German doctors. For this reason, we do not think it appropriate to entrust him with the supervision of ethnic Germans.'[23] It was then that Helmy learnt a new word. In order to make the distinction between Muslims and Jews, another racist label was needed. According to the Book of Genesis, all human beings are descended from the three sons of the prophet Noah: Shem, Ham, and Japheth. On this basis, the racial pseudoscientists came up with the term 'Hamites', by analogy with the Jewish 'Semites'.

A young colleague of Helmy's—one of the dashing, jackbooted sort—brought the new term into circulation at the hospital. Behind his supervisor's back, he went from room to room asking colleagues to sign a petition stating that they were no longer willing to stand by and let Dr Helmy, 'a Hamite', treat German women.[24]

Such was the plight of the once so promising parvenu Helmy when he got the call from Anna's grandmother, the owner of the greengrocer's on the Alexanderplatz. By now, in 1936, it was common knowledge that this 'Hamite' was blatantly continuing to treat Jewish patients over the heads of his staunchly anti-Semitic colleagues. Helmy took time for these patients, driving out to see them in his car—all during official working hours, needless to say. Indeed, he soon began to visit Anna's family on a regular basis.

Helmy had acquired his professional privileges as a senior physician on the back of Nazi hopes that he, as a Muslim, would side with them against the Jews. In the event, he subverted their plan, using those very privileges to help Jews. It was his secret revenge on the hospital's SS doctors: he was better than all of them, and he wasn't going to let them beat him. Thus, his help mission was partly motivated by the desire to get even, along with an intellectual urge for self-preservation.

Not only did he help his Jewish patients by alleviating their abdominal pains and breathing problems: he also assisted them in circumventing Nazi laws. For instance, he hid valuables from the prying eyes of the state, which was constantly inventing new taxes on Jews. For Anna's grandmother, he managed to send two hundred British pounds abroad;[25] for others, he took various items—eight hundred American dollars here, a small diamond there—into safekeeping.[26]

Whenever his Nazi colleagues attempted to put him under pressure, Helmy responded with the counter-threat that, if he were dismissed from his post, there would be political reprisals against German doctors working in Egypt.[27] His gamble paid off: the German Foreign Office continued to stand by him in its eagerness to keep him onside. Perhaps they genuinely feared an Egyptian revenge. Even if not, they clearly preferred to court the Muslim world rather than antagonize it. However much Helmy provoked his Brownshirt colleagues, the Foreign Office continued to give him the benefit of its protection. As time went on, the potential of this situation must have gradually dawned on Helmy.

The hospital management would have preferred to jettison Helmy at the earliest opportunity,[28] but the Ministry instructed it to be gracious toward the Muslim doctor and keep him on 'for foreign policy reasons'.[29] Even when the petition to stop the 'Hamite' from treating German women[30] was passed around the hospital, the Ministry continued to insist that it was more important to maintain good relations with the Muslim world.

Perhaps Helmy exaggerated somewhat when he boasted after the war of the liberties he took from this point onwards. Once, he claimed to have called Hitler a 'paralytic', and to have branded Göring a 'vain, short-sighted loudmouth' in front of the Nazi medical staff. When greeted with the words 'Heil Hitler!', he maintained—whether in the corridor or in his surgery—he would always reply with a plain 'good morning'.[31]

There was, Helmy later mischievously claimed, one exception to this rule, and that was 'on visiting the toilet'. There, even he—a Muslim—would make a point of greeting the Führer.[32]

# A STEP TOO FAR

The ground floor of the town house where Helmy lived—Krefelder Straße 7, Moabit—was occupied by a Jewish tobacconist, Markus Lesser. Above the shop, directly adjacent to Helmy, lived the Conitzers—Gertrud and Arthur—with their daughters Ursula and Ruth. The house belonged to the Jewish wine merchants Karoline and Feibusch Klag from Lemberg (now Lviv, Ukraine), and was used by the Nazis for 'densification measures', whereby evictees from other areas were moved into already occupied premises.

One of these was Erna Mendelsohn, a single woman from Königsberg (now Kaliningrad, Russia), whose home in the Altonaer Straße had been seized by the state. Another was Gertrud Bobert, the daughter of a cap manufacturer from the working-class district of Prenzlauer Berg. Her non-Jewish husband, a civil servant, had divorced her just as the race laws were being introduced in 1935, thus leaving her without protection.[1] The building had become crowded. Helmy was the only resident who had not been made to share his apartment with a stranger: only Jews had to take in Jews. But he saw at close quarters how life for Jews was changing all around them.

When Helmy's NSDAP and SA colleagues at the hospital finally succeeded in bringing about his departure, there was no big scene, no expulsion, just a small turn of the bureaucratic wheels. His contract simply ran out on 30 June 1937 and was not renewed. He may have been cleverer than them, but they were in the majority. From then on, Helmy had to earn his living privately, and therefore began to receive patients in his apartment in the Krefelder Straße, above Lesser's tobacconist's and next door to the Conitzers and Frau Mendelsohn.

Helmy practised 'more or less in secret', as he later stated, aided by his German partner, Emmy.[2] And just as the Jewish doctors of Moabit had once accepted him, a Muslim, into their midst, so he was now in a position to return the favour and take a Jewish girl under his wing by employing her as his assistant in this 'Jewish' house.

Anna, the girl from the Alexanderplatz, was by now fourteen years old. Her dream was to become a paediatric nurse. She had in mind a Jewish children's home in a suburb of the city, where her friend Regina Brauer, who was subsequently murdered, had also trained. But the home had since been closed by the Gestapo, and the Jewish community had warned Anna's mother that a similar fate was in store for the other training centres.[3] After the war, Anna remarked: 'It would be too long a story to list all the humiliations and persecution we Jewish children had to endure both in and outside school.'[4] She had had to switch to a Jewish school with a walled playground that backed directly onto the synagogue in the Oranienburger Straße.[5] The synagogue had a gold, ornamented Moorish dome that was once beautiful but, since 9 November 1938—shortly after Anna had begun her eighth and final year at school—the building had become a charred, blackened mess of metal struts and shards overshadowing the schoolyard.

Helmy had been impressed from the outset by Anna's unaffected, pragmatic manner—so different from those highly strung businesswomen, her mother and grandmother. The girl was bright and diplomatic. Helmy taught her how to analyse blood and urine samples under a microscope. And it didn't matter that, as a Jew, she was forbidden from treating 'Aryans',[6] since the mostly Jewish patients who came to his home were those who could no longer go to other doctors anyway.

After the war, Anna reported that Helmy also helped the Conitzers, as well as the Oppenheimers and the Bernatzkys, who came to him specially from the Klopstockstraße by the Tiergarten.[7] The details are somewhat hazy: was his assistance purely of a medical nature? Or did he also help the families to escape persecution by means of illegal actions, as Anna hinted in her post-war account?[8]

What is clear is that—just as he had done at the Robert Koch Hospital—Helmy continued to take astonishing liberties with the Nazis in his new role as a freelancer. On one occasion, leaving Anna alone at the practice, he strutted boldly into the Foreign Office building on Wilhelmstraße and up the stairs to the top floor, where he sought out the Middle East envoy Werner Otto von Hentig, a puffed-up, old-school aristocrat.

There, Helmy put his complaint to the diplomat, calling it a scandal that his medical career should be cut short in such a way, and demanding the right to confront one of the Hess brothers—if not Hitler's deputy Rudolf Hess, then at least his younger brother Alfred, vice-chief of the Nazi Party's Foreign Organization in Cairo.[9]

The stunned envoy asked in his turn whether what he had heard from Moabit hospital was true—that Helmy was spreading rumours that the Führer's deputy, Rudolf Hess, was an idiot?

No, certainly not, Helmy replied. He hadn't said that Hess was an idiot, or that he had been a failure at school, or that he was a moron. It was all a misunderstanding, and that was precisely why he needed to talk to Hess in person.[10]

The ministerial staff must surely have found it peculiar that this cocky young Egyptian—not yet forty, and already a specialist in kidney and bladder diseases[11]—should burst in here demanding interviews. Were they deceived into thinking that there might be a genuine reason behind his commanding, self-assured perform-ance? Perhaps they weren't entirely sure of their own ground. Relations with the Arab world in general and the British 'protec-torate' of Egypt in particular had begun to shift, especially since the outbreak of war. Moreover, the Nazi diplomats knew little of Helmy's military family in Cairo except that his father was a major and his brothers were officers.

It was true that Hitler's deputy, Hess, and his brother had grown up in Egypt. As sons of a German businessman, they had spent their early years in the port of Alexandria, a 'little paradise', as Rudolf Hess later called it. It was also quite possible that Hess and Dr Helmy had crossed paths in Berlin, as the deputy was a hypo-chondriac who had been in and out of Moabit hospital—now the hospital of choice for the Nazi elite. Hess even spoke a little Arabic, and his parents had once chided their sons for picking up swear words from the servants in Alexandria.[12]

Helmy may have been right to insist that he had never really claimed to have attended the same Egyptian school as Hess, or called him a moron or any such thing, and that it was all malicious gossip.[13] But then again, what did it matter whether he poked fun at this or that minister of Hitler's cabinet, be it Hess the school failure, Hitler the 'paralytic', or Göring the 'loudmouth'?[14] Helmy was determined to help his Jewish neighbours, patients, and friends—even, it seemed, if it meant circumventing the law. What's more, after years of protection from the Foreign Office, he spoke brazenly and apparently without fear in public. He acted provocatively, as if no one could touch him. Perhaps some Nazis were even impressed by him. Helmy, the offspring of a powerful military family, knew exactly which tone to take with them. The Middle East envoy was left speechless.

The same could not be said of the Hess brothers. Alfred Hess flew into a rage, informing the Berlin Gestapo 'in no uncertain terms' that this sneering Egyptian was a 'most unpleasant character',[15] and that he would be ready to 'make a detailed statement on the matter' at any time if required.[16] The elder Hess brother, Hitler's deputy, now also took a 'personal' interest in the private doctor from Berlin, as the Foreign Office noted.[17] 'At the express request of the Führer's deputy,' one memo read, 'Mohamed Helmy is to be prohibited from continuing his medical practice.'[18]

The younger brother, Alfred Hess, had just arrived abruptly in Berlin. It was September 1939, and he had fled to the city after being interned in Cairo by the British for a couple of days on the outbreak of war.[19] Back in Germany, he had bumped into Helmy in the street and been greeted by him.

Apoplectic, Hess went straight to the Secretary of State at the Foreign Office, Ernst von Weizsäcker—father of the subsequent German President. How was it possible, he expostulated, that Germans were being locked up in Cairo while an insolent Oriental like Helmy was free to walk the streets of Berlin?[20]

It was a Saturday. Weizsäcker rang the envoy at home and summoned him to the Ministry on the double. Fifteen minutes later, they were in conference. The upshot was that, in retaliation for the arrest of German nationals in the three British-controlled countries of Egypt, Palestine, and South Africa, approximately ten citizens of each of those countries currently resident in Germany would be interned with immediate effect.[21] Helmy, the overbearing foreigner with his mocking tales of Rudolf Hess's schooldays, would be top of the list. The piece of paper sealing his fate was stamped 'Very Urgent'.[22]

# GOING UNDERGROUND

The greengrocer's on the ground floor was gone: driving past, Helmy could only see dark window panes where the crates of peaches and strawberries had once been. The familiar stairs creaked ominously as he climbed to the second floor. It was 1942, a full six years after his first visit here to see Anna's grandmother. Two years had passed since his arrest by the Gestapo; after months of imprisonment, he had found himself at liberty again.

There was little left of the apartment's Wilhelminian interior. The armchairs, the Persian rugs, the wall mirror or trumeau, as the old lady liked to call it, had all been sold. The half-empty rooms were dingy and bleak.

Helmy, too, seemed changed. Nothing had been heard of him since his arrest shortly after the beginning of the war in autumn 1939, and Anna's family were puzzled by certain aspects of his story. He was well nourished and well dressed, and evidently had access to money again. As he himself explained, the state had given him a new—and indeed much better—practice of his own. A smart address in the Charlottenburg district, with no personal risk involved. All he had to do was turn up: the patients were already there.

But how exactly had he managed to get out of prison?, the women wanted to know. Helmy didn't give a straight answer.

Anna's grandmother regarded him with suspicion. But desperation made her put aside her reservations and turn to the doctor, their old acquaintance.

The deportation of Berlin's Jews had begun on 18 October 1941. From 21 December 1941, they were forbidden to use public telephones, and from 17 February 1942 they were no longer allowed to buy newspapers or magazines or visit 'Aryan' barbers. Today—Thursday, 5 March 1942—felt like the last straw for Anna's grandmother. In her hand was a letter from the Gestapo, addressed to Mrs Cecilie Sara Rudnik, as she was officially known. She was to pack a few things and report to the Moabit synagogue on Levetzowstraße, where the 'Reich Association of Jews in Germany' had been ordered by the authorities to set up a camp for several hundred people. The pews had been ripped out and the floor spread with straw. Trucks waited in the courtyard and, five miles away at Grunewald station, the cattle cars stood ready.

Anna's grandmother had only just returned from three weeks' imprisonment by the Gestapo for alleged contempt of Nazi government measures. She had been held in the basement of the police headquarters on the Alexanderplatz—a monstrous red-brick complex known as the 'Red Castle', from where, in the early days, the cries of torture victims sometimes reached the square.[1] I won't survive it a second time, she begged Helmy. But what was a sixty-seven-year-old widow to do? Flee the city? Go underground?

To her surprise, Helmy gave a clear diagnosis:[2] she should open her eyes, quit hoping, and go into hiding. Years later, Anna would recall how Helmy's words galvanized her grandmother into action: 'He was the one who persuaded her to get away and avoid capture'; to do otherwise would have been fatal.[3]

There was no time to lose, Helmy urged Cecilie. She should not give a moment's credence to the Gestapo's assurances that she would be taken to the eastern territories in order to work and make a new life for herself.

Cecilie hesitated for an instant, plucking up courage,[4] then hastily packed a single bag. Her loyal steward and office manager, Otto Buja,[5] found her lodgings for the first night via a contact in the city's Lichterfelde district.[6] But she couldn't stay there long. What she needed was a permanent hiding place in Berlin. Once again, it was Helmy who came up with the solution. He appealed to a former patient, Frieda Szturmann, a discreet homeworker and keen tarot reader from Staaken, near Spandau.[7] She was someone he could trust.

To allay Cecilie's misgivings, Helmy told her about the time he and his fellow Egyptians had spent in Gestapo custody from autumn 1939 onwards. He didn't tell her everything, just the early part: 'They handcuffed us and took us to proper jails, where we had to sleep on wooden surfaces and bare floors.' Later, he and his compatriots had been transferred to prisoner wagon cells and transported onward for days in the bitterest of conditions.[8] They were then imprisoned again in the medieval fortress of Wülzburg in Franconia, where Charles de Gaulle had once been interned in the First World War.[9]

The Nazis' reason for detaining the Egyptians was not to punish them, and certainly not to destroy them. As their victims soon realized, they had something else in mind: a prisoner exchange. This proved Helmy's salvation. In order to force the release of the Germans interned in Cairo, the Foreign Office had selected ten Egyptians resident in Germany who they deemed to have a

**Fig. 5.** Like many other Jewish business people, Anna's family lost their store in 1938 due to 'Aryanization'

particularly high exchange value.[10] The Foreign Office instructions to the Gestapo were to 'always intern the key figures first'.[11]

Beside the sneering senior physician Helmy, these included, among others, Dr Bey Aziz Cotta, the head of the German–Egyptian Chamber of Commerce; Riad Ahmed Mohamed,[12] the President of the Islamic community; Abdul Aziz Soliman, a ballet master from the Kurfürstendamm; and Zaki Halim, the son of an Egyptian prince. All educated, worldly individuals who made common cause in prison and—to the detriment of the Nazis—soon began to put their heads together.

Following Helmy's provocative swipes at the Nazi leadership at Moabit hospital, Wilhelm Bohle, State Secretary in the Foreign

Office, had deemed it imperative that Helmy in particular should remain locked up 'until the Egyptians have released every last citizen of the Reich'.[13] Helmy was not maltreated in prison, however, but handled comparatively humanely, as a political bargaining chip that was too valuable to lose.

At the beginning of May 1940, the Foreign Office had released all the prisoners again, including Helmy. Not because the Egyptians had met any political demands:[14] indeed, the number of Germans interned in Cairo had risen rather than fallen. The threat from Berlin had fallen completely flat, and had impressed no one in Cairo. And yet the Nazi diplomats had seen a reason to back down.

As the Foreign Office saw it, there was nothing to be gained by making long-term enemies of these prominent Muslim prisoners. If, instead of detaining them indefinitely, these 'key figures' of Berlin Muslim life could be won over to the Nazi regime by a gracious gesture, perhaps they could be turned into allies. Of all foreigners, they were, after all, the ones 'most suitable for propaganda purposes'.[15]

Any Muslim detainee who showed signs of being willing to cooperate with the regime found a ready ear in the Nazi leadership. Indeed, in at least one case—that of Mohamed Taufik Migahid, a twenty-one-year-old medical student and one of Helmy's fellow prisoners—the individual concerned was detained precisely with that goal in mind. Goebbels's propaganda ministry was looking for a presenter for Arabic radio broadcasts, and his people had taken a liking to the student's voice. The chilly prison walls had made the young man hoarse, however, and he was therefore left to stew until his vocal cords had recovered enough for test recordings—a prisoner of his cold as well as of the Nazis.[16]

Once released, Helmy had reason to fear for his freedom. The protection he enjoyed in Berlin depended on the Nazis regarding him as a new-found friend of the regime. Though once again at liberty, he—along with his fellow detainees—was not allowed to leave Germany. Alfred Hess, the rabid Nazi vice-chief in Cairo, had insisted on this because of the potential need to 'make further use of the individuals in question depending on political developments'—and also because they would need to be monitored 'due to the risk of espionage'.[17] For a while, therefore, Helmy had to report to the police every morning and afternoon.[18]

Nevertheless, he was evidently willing to risk this small, fragile measure of security for the sake of Anna's Jewish family by helping them again, as in the past, to circumvent laws and orders. It was a decision that would have serious consequences, as Anna later reflected, as it led the doctor to 'burden himself with the first catastrophe'.[19]

Cecilie had already stolen away to her first hiding place when Anna's stepfather came home from work at dusk to find her gone. According to Anna's account,[20] he 'went berserk' at the news.

Anna had never been able to endure her stepfather. To her, the man her mother Julie had taken as her second husband in 1929 would always be 'Fatty', or at best 'Uncle Wehr', but never Georg.[21] This short, balding man[22]—so quick-tempered that he could blow up at any moment, as the family knew only too well[23]—was not Jewish himself,[24] but had experienced at first hand the consequences of trying to hoodwink the Gestapo.

Nowadays, he trod carefully, and therefore disagreed with Helmy's advice to disobey the authorities. Perhaps he was also peeved that the women of the family had heeded it without even consulting him. He knew that, whenever the Gestapo tracked down missing Jews and dragged them from their hiding places, the first place they took them to was a house on the right bank of the Spree, Burgstraße 28. It was from the first and second floors of this building that the orders went out to arrest and deport Jewish Berliners to concentration camps. In the basement and second courtyard building, Jews were tortured and murdered in order to extract the names of their helpers and accessories,[25] who would then find themselves likewise in mortal danger. If you weren't Jewish yourself, sticking your neck out to help Jewish people could only end in tears.

The first time Anna's grandmother had turned to her son-in-law was in 1938, when the Nazi district office, in the shape of its 'economic advisor' Dr Müller, had contacted them to announce that the family greengrocery was to be 'Aryanized'. Cecilie had tried to persuade Georg—who already worked for the family business as cashier[26]—to take it over. The plan came to nothing, however: not only did the official make it clear that transferral to an 'Aryan son-in-law' would not be accepted,[27] but Georg Wehr was made to regret ever having been willing to help his in-laws. Müller promptly seized the family business, in the July of that same year. He then sold it to a company called Transdanubia GmbH, which paid a paltry 9,500 marks for it—approximately one week's turnover—only to liquidate it under the nose of the family upstairs.[28] And there was worse to come for Georg Wehr.

'Everyone knew about my circumstances', Wehr later reflected. 'No one wanted to be seen as a friend of the Jews'[29]—that is, someone like him. He remained unemployed for a year: no one would take him on since Müller had expressly testified to his lack of 'personal reliability'.[30] It was not until 1939 that Wehr managed to find another job, working for an old acquaintance who had a sausage meat factory in Lichterfelde.[31]

So what now? They couldn't lie to the Gestapo again, he remonstrated anxiously with Anna's mother, Julie. Better to keep a low profile, stick to the rules, keep their heads down—that way they would no longer be vulnerable to attack. The fact that Wehr— who could have betrayed the whole family—was pointedly packing his suitcase[32] during this altercation could have been seen as a threat. But, as so often, Anna's mother seemed not to realize the gravity of the situation. Anna, by then sixteen, later recalled how horror-struck she had been that evening.

'After much coaxing from us', she relates, Georg Wehr agreed to at least telephone Helmy. This gave Helmy the chance to spell out to her stepfather what was at stake for his Jewish family and thus deter him from abandoning them to their fate. They couldn't discuss the subject over the phone due to the risk of bugging, Anna explains. 'The doctor managed to calm my stepfather down, and told him to come over so that they could talk it through.'[33] As a consequence of all this, 'the doctor was now risking life and limb for everyone. Whether it was treating diseases, seeking new quarters or getting around the latest regulations, he had to keep on finding new solutions. My stepfather simply wasn't capable of doing it himself.'[34]

From then on, things moved fast. After Cecilie went into hiding, she was immediately followed by a second member of the family: her son from her first marriage, or Anna's half-uncle. Aged just twenty-four, Martin Rudnik was an extremely handsome man with a slew of female acquaintances, a fact that he was now able to use to his advantage. He found lodgings with two of these— Hildegard Ullbrich and her sister-in-law Irmgard—at 51a

Babelsberger Straße in Wilmersdorf, just a few minutes' walk from the twin minarets of the mosque.[35] The family home above the old greengrocer's was now finally empty. Helmy's strong words to Anna's family had had their effect.

Anna liked her charming uncle Martin, with whom she had much in common. Like Anna, he too was interested in medicine. In 1938, he had begun an apprenticeship as a dental technician with a Dr Grünbaum who, according to the new regulations, was no longer permitted to use the professional designation *Zahnarzt*, but only the lesser title *Dentist*.[36]

There, he had trained in rubber, metal, and bridge techniques and learned how to make dentures using Paladon.[37] Then the Nazis had tightened the laws even further and, in February 1939, Martin had to abandon his apprenticeship. In November 1941, he simply ceased to appear at the sheet metal factory in Weissensee where he had been conscripted for forced labour.[38] Otherwise he could have been deported from there at any moment, and he had no intention of making things that easy for his persecutors.

From then on, he lived as a cohabitant of the Ullbrichs, without ration cards. According to Anna, he got by, as had long been his wont, by engaging in 'all kinds of wheeling and dealing under a false identity'. One minute he was selling silk thread from Prague on the black market, the next it was cigarettes from Athens that Hildegard had been given by *Wehrmacht* soldiers.[39] Being a resourceful character, Martin had deposited various items of value with one acquaintance or another and was now gradually selling them off: a Leica camera, a valuable ring belonging to his late father, a gold pocket watch.[40] Now and then Otto Buja, Cecilie's faithful assistant, would also bring him money or cigarettes,[41] 'and whenever Martin was desperate', as Anna's mother remembered later, 'he would ring the doctor, who always knew what to do'.[42]

When the Gestapo came knocking for Cecilie at six in the morning, they were told that she had 'gone away'.[43] And so they took Anna with them for the time being—perhaps in order to make her parents talk. Anna was always reticent about this episode in later life, saying merely that she was questioned by the Gestapo officers, who warned her to leave Germany at once. 'If I ignored this instruction, I would be sent to the appropriate place.'[44]

Helmy realized what a close shave this had been for Anna, and how precarious the girl's situation was. And he had seen for himself after the bust-up with Georg Wehr how little help her parents would be. She needed a hiding place.

# A DARING PLAN

Like an outsider, Anna could observe the scene while remaining incognito. When she walked the streets alone, no one knew she was Jewish. She was the only one in her family who didn't wear a yellow badge. She didn't have to. Once, the district police chief, a Captain Ludwig, had told her to wear one, but Anna had never seen any reason to follow this instruction.[1]

Whenever she went from the Alexanderplatz to the embassy quarter by the Tiergarten—on foot, because Jews were not allowed to use the U-Bahn, and a long way round because Jews were banned from the area around the Brandenburg Gate—she passed people with the yellow patch on their coat. How easy it was to slip into someone else's skin, Anna sometimes thought; how readily one person could be taken for another! You could become invisible without having to hide. What did people think about her, she wondered, when they saw her pass by?

She had come to Berlin at the age of two, but had never taken German citizenship. For that reason, she had so far been exempted from 'security policy measures' such as the Jewish badge, even though her passport had been stamped with a 'J' since spring 1941. Her mother and grandmother had adopted the nationality of their German husbands: Anna's mother, newly divorced, had married the choleric Georg Wehr, and her grandmother, then a first-time widow, the amiable Jewish greengrocer Moise Rudnik. Anna had remained a foreigner, having been born in Arad, on the border between Hungary and Romania.

Consequently, when the Gestapo began to deport Jews from Berlin, Anna had not—unlike her grandmother—been summoned to the assembly point at the Levetzowstraße synagogue, but to the Romanian Consulate instead. As she relates, 'all foreigners were told to get out'.[2] The Gestapo had written to Anna instructing her to get her passport stamped at the Consulate and leave Germany for Romania within three days. Although Anna had no intention of complying with this order,[3] she saw what happened to other foreign Jews who refused. 'The other poor wretches were locked up', Anna writes. 'They would have locked me up too if I hadn't...disappeared in time.'[4]

The Consulate was a three-storey mansion with a black-painted iron fence. Anna held out the small blue booklet embossed with the words *Regatul Romaniei, Pasaport pentru strainatate* in gold lettering: Kingdom of Romania, Foreigner Passport. It was March 1942. For a while, a Romanian passport had afforded Jews some measure of protection. Now it was worthless: in November 1941, the Romanian government had verbally approved the German Reich's plan to include Romanian Jews in its extermination programme. It no longer had any interest, it said, in returning them to Romania.[5]

The Consular official behind the fence was friendly. As he stamped Anna's passport, he advised her not to travel to Romania under any circumstances. She would never get there; it would mean certain death.[6] 'I was left with no choice but to go into hiding,'[7] Anna explains. 'We had already heard that the Jews weren't being sent to Romania, but to camps in Poland.'[8]

Anna talked to Dr Helmy about possible hiding places. Staying with Helmy's obliging patient Frieda Szturmann was no longer an option. The poor woman had enough on her plate since taking in Cecilie. 'My grandmother would never hold her peace: wherever she went, she ended up quarrelling with the host family', Anna writes,[9] recalling her feelings of exasperation. Even after the war, the memory filled her with anger: 'She was so spiteful and rude—she just couldn't keep her damned mouth shut. She was a liability to the people who gave her shelter. And it was always the doctor who had to take responsibility and find a solution.'[10] Thus, Anna was deprived of another possible escape route.

Cecilie had been a businesswoman all her life. She had had to drive a hard bargain and stick up for herself, otherwise she would probably never have survived in the Berlin business world. She had always prided herself on her 'iron discipline' and 'extreme thrift'.[11] How, then, could such a woman, perpetually fretting lest the young people should starve in her absence,[12] be expected to cope in her new hideaway at Frieda Szturmann's sister's, where she was not allowed to make a sound for fear of alerting the neighbours?[13] It was quite a comedown: only a few years since, the sixty-seven-year-old Cecilie Rudnik had been mistress of a large international business and matriarch of a rich family. Now she was forced to keep as still as a mouse.

And what of Martin, Anna's young uncle? He too did 'absolutely nothing' to help Anna, as her mother later bitterly reflected. Despite his flourishing black-market trade and numerous contacts, he only looked after himself. Anna's mother was appalled. 'Eventually', she remarked ruefully, Martin 'lost touch' with them.[14] Some families may have grown closer together in those difficult times, but theirs wasn't one of them.

Anna's story continues: 'Then I was pursued by the Gestapo.'[15] Where else could she go? Furious with her grandmother and uncle and disappointed in her mother, she turned to Helmy.

Sometimes a beguiling thought would occur to Anna in the street: what if she pretended to be someone else? That way she could disappear in broad daylight, hidden, as it were, in plain sight. Helmy looked at Anna: she had her mother's dark hair, and her dark eyes radiated energy. She was no longer a child, but a young woman—even if her cheeks still dimpled when she smiled.

When did Anna's fantasy turn into a concrete plan? Perhaps Helmy told her the details of the deal he had struck with the regime as a prisoner in 1939/40. He had got his own practice again, at Kaiser-Friedrich-Straße 7, Charlottenburg, replacing Dr Wedekind, a German physician who had since been called up. Consequently, he had regained certain freedoms, a place in bourgeois society, and the right to issue prescriptions and medical certificates.

All that was missing was a receptionist. It couldn't be a Jewish one this time, of course, as Jews were no longer allowed to treat 'Aryan' patients. But a Muslim one would pass muster all right. And that was how the Jewish Anna morphed overnight into the Muslim Nadia, the doctor's 'niece'.

That, at least, was how he presented her to his state-appointed minders in Charlottenburg. On 10 March 1942, the Gestapo was notified that the Jewish girl Anna had 'gone away'. Questioned by uniformed officials, Anna's mother and stepfather insisted that they had seen her personally onto the train to Romania, and even showed them a receipt for the ticket.[16] Anna was relieved to learn that they had evidently got away with this lie. 'The Gestapo didn't believe my parents' story, but they had no evidence to the contrary.'[17]

The name Nadia had been Helmy's idea. It was almost like an adoption. Perhaps you should start calling yourself Nadia mentally, he had suggested, the first time she reached for a scarf to cover her hair. That way you won't give yourself away. The new name meant 'morning dew' in Persian. In Arabic, it meant 'one who calls'. Anna was quite taken with it.[18]

# HIDDEN IN PLAIN SIGHT

In the morning, she would let the scarf sink onto her hair like a parachute before taking one end of the fabric and throwing it over her shoulder. Not that it was necessary, of course. But it was a good idea, as Anna soon realized. It was astonishing how the scarf diverted people's attention from her face. It worked like a magic cloak.[1] When people saw it, they noticed very little else about her.

Anna drove to work with her protector in the morning and home again in the evening, never straying from his side. If anyone asked too many questions, he could answer for her. When uniformed patrol officers stopped the car and ordered them to wind down the window and present their papers, Dr Helmy would look at them with studied irritation: didn't they know they were dealing with a friend of the Foreign Office?[2] Surely they could see that he was an Arab—of all foreigners, the 'most suitable for propaganda purposes',[3] as the ministerial staff had crowed?

He would then take his national identity card from his pocket, a colour-printed document issued by the Royal Embassy of Egypt. For his 'niece' Nadia, he presumably obtained a falsified document—perhaps belonging to a daughter of one of the Muslim diplomats who were now gradually leaving the capital in the wake of the war. What Anna needed was an ID showing a fair-skinned

**Fig. 6.** Children being taught in the garden of the Berlin mosque

girl with dark curly hair. That might be enough, especially given the Gestapo's unfamiliarity with Egyptian papers, plus the fact that Arab families didn't necessarily share the same surname. Indeed, it was rare in Egypt for a woman to take her husband's name.

'My niece from Dresden', Helmy would say, indicating the young woman in the passenger seat and rolling his eyes, as if this was the umpteenth time he had had to explain it. Then he would usually point out——truthfully in this case——that he had medical duties to attend to. Sitting next to him, Anna would give an awkward, nervous smile as Helmy stepped on the gas and drove on to the practice in Charlottenburg.[4]

Keeping up Anna's pretence required the utmost concentration. Sometimes, Helmy would call over to her in Arabic, and she would make a show of understanding every word, calling back

'Yes!' and smiling at the patients in the waiting room. They fed each other lines. 'I learned a lot', Anna later wrote of this period of her life, full of admiration for Helmy's resourcefulness.[5] And Helmy was impressed in his turn by how quickly Anna picked things up.

Helmy, too, had to dissemble and act a part. In his dealings with the Gestapo, he now played the ideal pro-Nazi Arab envisioned by Goebbels's propaganda office: an Egyptian whose homeland had suffered under the detested British, just as the Rhineland had suffered under the detested French. An Egyptian whose dearest wish was to see Germany prevail over these old colonial powers.

According to an SS pamphlet aimed at the Muslim population of Bosnia in particular, the Allies had an interest in 'killing as many Muslims as possible'. And the Nazi propaganda didn't stop there: it went on to remind Muslims that 232 million of their number lived 'under English, American, French, and Russian foreign rule'. Needless to say, it didn't mention that the Germans harboured the same colonial ambitions. On the contrary: it claimed that only Germany had true respect for Islam. 'If Germany is defeated, the last hope for you Muslims ever to become free also fades.'[6]

Helmy could throw himself whole-heartedly behind these sentiments when he needed to. Indeed, that was the secret of the good relations he now maintained with the regime. No longer did he make gleeful swipes at Nazi bigwigs such as Hess, Hitler, and Göring, calling them 'paralytics' or 'loudmouths'. Instead, he made an outward show of absolute loyalty to Hitler—an act he had perfected in Gestapo custody, together with his Egyptian friends: the ballet master, the chairman of the Chamber of Commerce, the prince's son, and the president of the Islamic association.

This was the part Helmy had omitted to tell Anna's suspicious grandmother, just in case. Even from his prison cell in 1939, he had actively sought contact with the regime, and had begun to write unctuous letters to the Nazi top brass in fulsome, obsequious tones. One of these was directed to Hitler himself, whom he addressed as 'your Excellency'.

In it, Helmy had claimed to have 'campaigned actively for the National Socialist movement since 1929' and been 'injured in an attack by its adversaries in 1931'. Helmy had fed the dictator the sob story of a long-suffering champion of the Nazi cause. He—a Muslim—had even had to work without pay until 1933, and had been denied a post as a doctor simply because he was too anti-Semitic for the Nazi-hating Jewish bosses of Moabit hospital.[7]

This was a blatant falsehood. The three unpaid years after his degree were the normal length of time taken by young doctors to earn their spurs. During this period, Helmy—who was friends with Jewish doctors and lived among Jewish families—had been paid in kind by his Jewish bosses, receiving free food and lodging like all other junior doctors. But Helmy lied through his teeth and told the Nazis whatever they wanted to hear. His Egyptian jail-mates tried the same trick, and they rejoiced together at the readiness of the regime to take the bait. Helmy was most likely amazed himself at how well it worked at first.

While in Gestapo custody, he had already approached the Nazis—who still had their sights set on a prisoner exchange—offering to use his allegedly good connections in Egypt to procure the release of the Germans interned in Cairo. The only proviso was that he and one other Egyptian prisoner be released in return. This friend, the long-time chairman of the German–Egyptian Chamber of Commerce, Dr Cotta, had lived in Germany for many years, had three children with a woman from Düsseldorf, and was the owner of a cinema chain.

Helmy's proposal had created quite a buzz at the Foreign Office. Following a personal telephone call between the Foreign Minister and Rudolf Hess's chief of staff, Martin Bormann, Helmy and Cotta were promptly freed at the beginning of December 1939, 'on condition that they obtain the release of the Germans interned in Egypt',[8] by 'leveraging their influence and connections', as the Foreign Office added expectantly.[9] They were given thirty days.

Needless to say, Christmas, New Year 1939/1940 and the entire thirty days elapsed without Helmy pulling any strings or activating any channels. In reality, he didn't even have good relations with his own family in Cairo, let alone with politicians. And in reality, he had remained an anti-Nazi, despite his successful play-acting. Consequently, the number of Germans interned in Egypt did not fall during the thirty days; in fact it rose, rendering the whole episode even more absurd.

The diplomats at the Foreign Office were left with egg on their faces, and had Helmy and the cinema owner rearrested when the thirty days were up.[10] But Helmy continued to insist even more emphatically on his support for the Nazi regime. In 1939, he told the Foreign Office that he had been a member of the Party for ten years—the 'only Egyptian' among their ranks.[11] Muslims were expressly welcome, the Party had once declared: indeed, it invited their participation. 'Germans belonging to the Islamic faith' had 'just as much right to be members of the NSDAP as those belonging to Christian denominations', Hitler's Party Secretary Martin Bormann once clarified in a memorandum.[12]

In fact, Helmy had never joined the NSDAP. This particular falsehood was a major gamble, and, since the Foreign Office promptly contacted the regional Party headquarters to inquire about him,[13] it was soon exposed. Astonishingly, however, they let it go unpunished. Perhaps the officials gladly turned a blind eye to the fabrications of this pro-German zealot, who was probably just trying too hard. So eager were they to win Muslim loyalty, the Nazi strategists may even have deemed it an advantage that this one was willing to sacrifice the truth in order to get into their good books.

Some of Helmy's Muslim acquaintances did similar things for their own ends. Happy to be courted and flattered, they earned money by translating propaganda pamphlets or passages from *Mein Kampf*, albeit with certain omissions: when questioned, fifteen years on, about the book's rantings against the Muslim 'coalition of cripples', Hitler agreed that 'those parts should be omitted which appear unsuitable for translation in view of the current political situation and the sensitivity of Arab nations'.[14]

Helmy was not the only Muslim in Berlin who began to string the regime along. Outwardly at least, they all played the Nazis' game. In his standard sermon 'What has Islam given humanity?', for instance, the imam of the Wilmersdorf mosque, Dr Abdullah, summarily substituted the term 'ethnic community' for the word 'democracy'.[15] In the *Moslemische Revue*, he increasingly gave a platform to those who—to the delight of the propaganda ministry— claimed to see parallels between Islam and Nazism.[16]

In some cases, this deference was genuine. The mosque community was gradually becoming dominated by German converts to Islam like Fritz 'Hikmet' Beyer, who belonged to Nazi organizations for ideological reasons, and the majority on the executive committee was shifting accordingly. In other cases, however, it was a sham, as in the case of the Jewish writer Hugo 'Hamid'

Marcus, who managed by this means to stay on as manager of the mosque until 1935.

Even after 1935, the mosque continued to entrust Marcus with the translation and annotation of the Quran, supporting him financially and, in 1938, secretly procuring him visas for Muslim Albania and British India.[17] He was already living in exile when his translation of the Quran was collected from the printers in 1939 and proudly presented in Berlin. For tactical reasons, this first-ever translation 'from the pen of a Muslim' had to be attributed to other people.[18]

When Anna looked up at Helmy, she saw a man old enough to have been her father. Her real father, Ladislaus Boros, had once promised, after divorcing her mother in Romania, to visit his daughter twice a year. In fact, she only ever saw him once in Berlin, when she was three years old.[19] At Helmy's, she was now well provided for, with a room of her own. A keen cook, she took charge of the kitchen chores[20] and was good at crafts such as sewing and knitting.[21] What's more, she got along well with the third member of the household, Helmy's fiancée, Emmy. Emmy had become engaged to Helmy at the age of twenty-three, but was already twenty-six by the time Anna came to stay in 1942.

Emmy also played her part in the deception. She too had to ingratiate herself with those whom she would sooner have resisted. During Helmy's detention by the Gestapo, she had been extremely anxious about him, but he had briefed her on what to do—and she had leapt into the breach by concocting a letter in simulated Nazi style to Foreign Minister von Ribbentrop. 'Forgive me, your Excellency, for appealing most urgently to your Excellency to place the enclosed petition before our revered Führer', Emmy wrote, expressing the hope that Helmy would be spared on the grounds of his 'loyalty to the National Socialist government'.[22] The wording had been prearranged between the two of them. To Hitler, she wrote: 'Dr Helmy has been involved in political campaigning for the NSDAP since 1929, and was attacked on one occasion by its opponents ... Sieg Heil to you, my Führer!'[23]

As long as they could keep up the pretence that Helmy was among those Arabs sympathetic to the regime, he had a chance to save himself and protect Anna. As long as the façade endured, they could move around freely, even now that the deportation hub for Berlin's Jews had moved to their immediate vicinity. As of August 1942, the trains no longer departed from Grunewald freight yard, but from Moabit, just a few minutes' walk from Helmy's apartment.

On 15 August 1942—by which time Anna was already living with Helmy in Moabit—a trainload of 997 people had left here bound for Riga. Subsequent transports saw 796 deported to Riga on 5 September, 1,049 to Raasiku on 26 September, 959 to Riga on 19 October, and 798 to Riga on 26 October. The Jews were assembled, lined up, and sent to their deaths. It was a sight you couldn't avoid in Moabit. Sometimes, screaming and shouting could be heard. At the same time, the Gestapo manhunters were upping the pressure on Jewish fugitives by tracking down their meeting places and carrying out more and more raids.

From November 1942 onwards, the deportation trains had only one destination: Auschwitz. On 29 November 1942, 998 people were dispatched there from Moabit, followed by 994 on 9 December and 815 on 14 December; 1,196 were deported on 12 January 1943, 1,004 on 29 January, 952 on 13 February, 997 on 19 February, 913 on 26 February, 1,722 on 1 March, 1,756 on 2 March, 1,726 on 3 March, 1,120 on 4 March, 665 on 6 March, 941 on 12

March, 681 on 19 April, and 406 on 17 May. Whenever Anna left the house under her false identity, she never knew whether she would return. If someone from her former life were to recognize her on the street, they could betray her at any moment.

By now, the Gestapo had ceased to rely on denunciations from the community, having instead recruited a Jewish search service to help locate those in hiding. This consisted of poor wretches who betrayed others to save their own skin—only to end up being murdered themselves. So great was the persecutors' zeal that Fedor Friedländer, a notorious 'catcher', was said to have hunted down up to 300 fugitives single-handedly.[24]

For as long as their charade lasted, Helmy and Anna continued to perfect Anna's role as Nadia. And they went further still, pushing what liberties they had to the limits: after all, no one could say how long they would continue to enjoy them. Using the resources made available to them by the Nazis, the doctor and his receptionist also managed to rescue others.

At their Charlottenburg practice, they issued medical certificates for forced labourers, and certified Germans as too sick to be deployed for hard physical labour. Towards the end, they also pronounced some unfit to join the Volkssturm, the last-ditch defence when Berlin was in flames. And all the while they continued to treat Jews illegally in secret, a fact that did not escape the Gestapo's notice for long,[25] and was part of the reason for their intrusive visits. The doctor will be with you directly! 'Nadia' would reassure them pleasantly. One moment please, I will fetch the doctor for you.

Between them, they staged a high-risk performance as two Muslims loyal to the Nazi state. Nor was the danger over once the Gestapo overcame its suspicions and began to take them at their word: if anything, life became even more hazardous than before.

# IN THE LION'S DEN

The Prinz Albrecht Hotel had seen very different days. Though it had continued to host lavish parties up to 1932, its grand ballrooms were now idle, and the once opulent building was falling into disrepair. More than a hundred rooms and suites lay behind the elaborate art nouveau façade of this palatial residence, now patrolled by SS officers in black uniforms. It was from this building that SS chief Heinrich Himmler directed the extermination of Europe's Jews.

The Prinz-Albrecht-Straße led directly to the Wilhelmstraße, the power centre of the Third Reich, where the key ministries—including Hitler's Reich Chancellery—sat side by side, amid fluttering flags and dark columns of vehicles on the move. The SS had first installed itself here in 1934, taking over more state functions and appropriating more buildings with each passing year. Its terror and death camps spanned the whole of Europe, but its beating heart lay here. Nearly every basement was a torture chamber, and the streets were full of uniformed men. In short, this was probably the last place on earth you would seek to go if you were a Jewish fugitive in 1943. Or, for that matter, if you were hiding one.

One day, however, Dr Helmy and 'Nadia' were summoned by the SS to this very spot. How they must have felt on pulling up outside the hotel is hard to imagine. No one had told them exactly what the meeting was about—only that the doctor should bring his medical kit with him, along with his Muslim assistant.[1]

Light spilled through the old arcades on the hotel's first floor. The visitors filled out the requisite form for the SS guard, then took the lift as instructed. When the doors opened, they were confronted with a curious scene.

Before them stood a crowd of men engrossed in conversation. The focus of their attention was a small gentleman with reddish hair, a full beard, and blue eyes. This fifty-or-so-year-old Palestinian—none other than the Grand Mufti of Jerusalem, Amin al-Husseini—cut an imposing figure in his white fez and dark robe, and his entourage were dressed with similar elegance. Such an encounter was probably the last thing Anna and Helmy had expected. Since November 1941, the SS had been cultivating this delegation of several dozen men. They were guests of honour in Berlin—perhaps the most visible example of the Nazi charm offensive on the Muslim world—and Helmy and 'Nadia' had been invited in order to provide the gentlemen with medical care, from Muslim to Muslim.

Not that they had had any choice about venturing into this lion's den: how could they have refused a summons from the SS? The fact that they were asked here at all, however, was a sign of how well they were playing their role as pro-Nazi Muslims loyal to the regime. They had clearly failed to arouse any suspicion. So far, no one had uncovered Anna's masquerade.

The Grand Mufti of Jerusalem was a dangerous man for Jews. 'The Jews can be compared to disease-carrying insects', he proclaimed in one of his propaganda speeches. 'If they are far away, one can believe them to be peaceful creatures, but if a person is stung by them and afflicted with the illness, then only radical

**Fig. 7.** Heinrich Himmler greeting SS guest of honour the Grand Mufti of Jerusalem

remedies can help.'[2] The Grand Mufti's ideological affinity with the German anti-Semites was no pretence, but a genuinely held belief. And now Anna, who was merely acting the role of an Arabic-speaking Muslim, suddenly found herself standing just a few yards away from him.

The Grand Mufti had approached the Germans at an early stage. On the eve of 1 April 1933—the day the SA men had first begun to stand outside the Rudniks' shop on the Alexanderplatz shouting anti-Semitic slogans—he had extended his congratulations to the Reich ambassador. A boycott to 'target the wealth of the Jews', the Grand Mufti had declared appreciatively, would find enthusiastic support throughout the entire Muslim world.[3] He, as the representative of Palestinian Muslims, could only endorse this course of action by the Nazi government.

In Egypt, German troops were battling against Britain in the desert. In Iraq, the Anglophobic politician Rashid Ali al-Gailani had just staged a coup against the British, but fell from power after just a few weeks. Like the Grand Mufti, he too had fled to Berlin, but not before instigating a two-day pogrom in Baghdad in which some 200 Jews were killed and 900 houses destroyed—an event that was to go down in history as the *Farhud*. Both men were welcomed in Berlin, as the Nazi regime had an idea for making use of them.

The Grand Mufti had already made a name for himself. In autumn 1933, around the time when Helmy's colleague Dr Leffkowitz had fled to Palestine after the Nazi beatings, the Grand Mufti had spearheaded an Arab protest strike there against Jewish immigrants. The swastika was widely displayed on pamphlets and walls.[4] When the Grand Mufti eventually ran into trouble with Palestine's British administrators, he had fled—at times smooth-shaven and disguised in women's clothing—via a tortuous route across Iran and Turkey to Italy. From there, Hitler had arranged for him to fly to Berlin on 6 November 1941, a few days after the beginning of the Jewish deportations from the capital.

A fez is a short, cylindrical hat made from red felt with a tassel on top. It is hard to imagine a more impractical form of headgear for military purposes, as it is neither streamlined nor waterproof, let alone bullet-proof. On the plus side, it allows the wearer to touch the floor with their forehead during Muslim prayers. When a bulk order of these caps was delivered to the SS, in dark red with a black tassel and a metallic insignia on the front depicting the imperial eagle and death's head, the SS leader Himmler intervened personally. Apparently, he didn't like the design.

In a letter to his administrative chief Oswald Pohl—later executed in Nuremberg—Himmler complained that the fezzes needed to be 're-dyed and cut a bit shorter', in order to distinguish them sufficiently from the caps of the enemy Moroccans, who were known for wearing the tallest fezzes, albeit with neither an eagle nor a death's head. According to Himmler, 'These outward semblances are tremendously important for the stabilization of the division.'[5]

The caps were intended for use in the Balkans. During their invasion of the region in 1941, the German troops had recruited Muslim Albanians and Bosnians as accomplices in the hunt for Tito's Partisans. Now the SS was endeavouring in various ways to keep these men happy. In a curious departure from its usual policy, however, it chose to do this principally by reminding them of their religion and encouraging what the SS called the emergence of an Islamic identity among their ranks. The Germans urged the recruits to observe Muslim prayers, and field imams preached to them about Hitler, who the imam of the SS Bosnian Handschar Division described in a ceremonial address of 1943 as 'fighting for God, faith, morality, and a better and fairer world order'.[6]

It was for this kind of propaganda that the Nazis deployed the Grand Mufti of Jerusalem. He was to recruit Muslim volunteers and stir up Muslim populations via radio broadcasts. In return for his services, he was given an 'Aryanized' villa along with offices and residences in Berlin-Zehlendorf, at the Adlon Hotel and in the former Jewish Institute on Klopstockstraße. Further rewards included a lavish monthly allowance of 75,000 Reichsmarks, crack SS bodyguards, and the vague hope that Hitler would one day support his plan for an independent Palestine—preferably one in which he, the Grand Mufti, would be a figure with real power.[7]

Four of the six 'voluntary' legions that the Wehrmacht could draw on in the East were Muslim: a 25,000–38,000-strong Caucasian–Mohammedan legion, a 28,000-strong North Caucasian legion, a 35,000–40,000-strong Volga-Tatar legion, and a 110,000–180,000-strong Turkestan legion. Their badge bore the motto Biz Alla Bilen, 'Allah is with us', accompanied by a depiction of the Shah-i-Zinda mosque at Samarkand, one of the holiest sites for Central Asian Muslims. Three Muslim battalions fought on the German side in the battle of Stalingrad, and even as late into the war as autumn 1944 the SS withdrew its 1st Eastern Muslim Regiment temporarily from the Eastern Front to celebrate the end of Ramadan with a special sunrise service on 18 September.[8]

It is doubtful whether religion played much of a role in the motivation of these 'volunteers', however. They were prisoners of war, many of whom only wore the German uniform for their own protection. Nevertheless, the SS believed in the power of its religious propaganda. Himmler is said to have remarked that 'Islam is very similar to our world view'. Apparently, the SS leader was particularly taken with the cult of martyrdom and the seventy-two virgins supposedly awaiting every martyr, claiming, 'This is the kind of language a soldier understands.'[9]

Although Anna's alter ego Nadia was an Arab, she herself spoke no Arabic. Fortunately, her subsidiary role as Helmy's receptionist enabled her to remain in the background, and she stuck close to his side in order to avoid getting into conversation with one of the Arab gentlemen. The fact that girls like her were not expected to interfere in the discussions of grown-up men at the best of times may also have worked in her favour. Should one of the Mufti's staff speak to her, she could perhaps still get by using the story she and Helmy had agreed on for such an eventuality: that she had lived in Dresden since her childhood and, alas, never learned Arabic properly. Nevertheless, it must have been the biggest test of her acting ability so far. If she were to be asked any further questions, she would really have to think fast.

The Grand Mufti showed no mercy to Jewish children: quite the opposite. At the end of 1942, he protested against the German plan to allow 4,000 Jewish children from Slovakia, Poland, and Hungary to emigrate to Palestine under the auspices of the Red Cross in return for the release of German civilian internees. Over tea at the Prinz Albrecht Hotel, he had expressed his concerns to SS leader Himmler: in a few years' time, these children would be grown up, thus 'strengthening the Jewish element in Palestine'.[10] Following his intervention, the operation was duly stopped.

In August 1942, the Nazis dropped 296,000 pamphlets over Syria warning against a Jewish state, which, in the event of a British military victory, would occupy a large part of the Middle

East. The Grand Mufti took the same line in a radio address broadcast throughout the Arab world on the occasion of the Islamic New Year celebrations of 17 December 1944: 'We will not be satisfied with less than what the free nations have fought for—genuine independence that does not allow entry to foreigners and that leaves no room for Jews, in which the entire Arab fatherland is available to the Arab people alone.'[11]

Hitler had assured the Grand Mufti in Berlin that Germany's 'uncompromising struggle against the Jews' would 'include, of course, opposition to a Jewish homeland in Palestine, which is nothing more than a national hub for the destructive influence of Jewish interests'.[12] Despite this, the Mufti waited in vain for concrete commitments from the Nazis to support his plans for Palestine.

It was in the immediate vicinity of such a man that Anna now found herself. 'Fear is a word she never used when talking about her life', her son once remarked many years later, displaying not only admiration for his mother for riding out such a situation at the age of seventeen, but downright incredulity.[13] Perhaps it was Anna's capacity to keep her feelings to herself—the very characteristic that, in her childhood, had seemed to her a painful inability to talk to anyone about her innermost thoughts—that now saved her life.

# AN OVERNIGHT
# CONVERSION

The house in Moabit lay silent in the darkness. Even though there was no test to sit and no ceremony to perform, Anna was still nervous when the man Helmy had been waiting for knocked at the door that June night. The visitor, who was short and squat, with close-cropped white hair and a thin moustache above his top lip which, as a German reporter later wrote disparagingly, 'further underlined his mouse-like features',[1] was not unfamiliar to Anna. She had seen him once before: at the SS gathering in the Prinz Albrecht Hotel.

There, the man had whispered things in Arabic into the Grand Mufti's ear. Anna recalled his gestures precisely: the way he surreptitiously picked at his nose, blew out his cheeks, or placed a finger conspiratorially on his lips. He was the Grand Mufti's right-hand man, working at the very centre of anti-Semitic agitation. His name was Kamal el-Din Galal, and he was the General Secretary of the Islamic Central Institute of Berlin. Why on earth should we trust him?, Anna had asked her protector in horror.

For that very reason, Helmy had endeavoured to reassure her.

He had begun to work out a plan to provide Anna with a long-term escape route. This, her conversion to Islam on 10 June 1943, was to be the first step. The certificate to prove it had been obtained from the Islamic Central Institute, whose patron was none other than the Grand Mufti and Hitler supporter Amin al-Husseini. In Helmy's student days, it had been just one of many associations and discussion groups, and his friend Riad Ahmed Mohamed had sometimes chaired meetings in those camel-adorned premises gifted by the Kaiser. Six months ago, the institute had been officially 'reopened' in a new guise. A ceremony had been held, complete with bouquets of flowers, at the Prinz-Albrecht-Palais or 'House of Aviators', the building next to Himmler's SS headquarters.

At four thirty in the afternoon of 19 December 1942, the day of the sacrificial feast of Eid al-Adha, the Grand Mufti stepped up to the microphone, to be hailed as the 'leader of the Arab world', notably by diplomats and uniformed men with undercut hairstyles who had turned out in force.[2]

Needless to say, the Grand Mufti was not informed that he was about to sponsor the conversion of a Jewish girl to the Islamic faith. Helmy's plan depended on being able to smuggle her past him unnoticed. The Nazis cultivated such close relations with the Mufti that Helmy hoped they wouldn't probe into the background of alleged members of his congregation and, if they did, that they would perhaps turn a blind eye. Who would spot one Nadia more or less among the Muslim community?

That night, Helmy and Galal greeted each other quietly at the door of Helmy's apartment, in case the neighbours at number 7 Krefelder Straße should hear them through the thin walls.

They were old friends. Like Helmy, Galal was Egyptian. The two of them had come to Berlin together in 1922, fresh from school, and had learned German together as students. Then Galal had got into politics. Unlike Helmy, he had distinguished himself as a vociferous opponent of British colonial rule on the Nile. In Berlin, he had taken part in various protests, holding up placards in front of the British embassy and presenting petitions to the ambassador.[3]

An Arab agitating against the British was music to the Nazis' ears. They arranged for Galal to study journalism and 'racial ideology' (*völkische Erziehung*). Then, in 1939, they invited him to become editor of the magazine *Bariq al-Sharq* or 'Orient News', which was founded by the propaganda ministry and distributed mainly in the North African war zones and among prisoners of war.[4] Needless to say, they excluded Galal from the group of Arabs— among them Helmy—arrested in September 1939. At the time, the Foreign Office praised the propaganda writer, who was 'known to be reliable',[5] and considered 'beneficial' to the Nazi regime.[6] As such, he enjoyed protection. But he didn't forget his friends.

Galal had visited Helmy in Gestapo custody and pleaded for his release, albeit in vain. He was known as a friend of the Nazis, and had tried to convince them that Helmy was too, and that he should therefore be well treated.

Despite this, Galal was now willing to support Helmy's plan to help the Jewish girl—by night, using stolen letterheads and stamps. Helmy knew his friend long enough to know that he too was playing a role. Although he worked for the Grand Mufti, he didn't share the Mufti's anti-Semitism. Had he been a fanatic like his boss, who wished Jews dead from the heart, he would never have joined in the subterfuge.

One imagines a mood of quiet solemnity descending over the two old friends as they explained their plan to Anna. The apartment in Moabit was dark, the door locked, the curtains closed.

Perhaps they got Anna to recite the Islamic creed, the Shahada: La ilaha illa 'llah. Muhammadun rasulu 'llah.—There is no god but God. Muhammad is the messenger of God. Or perhaps they dispensed with it—the whole exercise was absurd enough already. In this case it was not a religious act they were performing, but a humanitarian one.

Helmy's fiancée, Emmy, had never shown any sign of wanting to convert to Islam, nor had Helmy ever shown any sign of loving her the less for it. Nevertheless, he would define himself as a Muslim throughout his life,[7] and he respected religious rituals. In his view, to simply parrot the words of the Shahada without meaning them would be to devalue them.

Anna's family had never been overly devout either. They had belonged to Berlin's Jewish community as a matter of course.[8] They had sung and raised a glass at Passover, the spring festival celebrating the exodus of the Hebrews from slavery in Egypt, led by Moses, the Jewish adoptive son of the Pharaoh family. They knew God's words to the Hebrews in the Torah: 'You know the soul of the stranger, for you were strangers in the land of Egypt'.

When it came to the feast, however, Anna's mother had sometimes served up Hungarian meatballs bound with milk. Very tasty, but about as far from kosher as you could get.[9] They had wished each other *Mazel tov*,[10] even though it was the wrong greeting for the occasion, meaning 'congratulations' rather than 'happy holiday'. And a few days later they would wish each other happy Easter.[11] That was how laid-back they were about the whole business.

And yet, equally, Anna would always define herself as Jewish throughout her life. Her Muslim protectors, Helmy and Galal, were well aware that her conversion to Islam that night was a complete sham, but they couldn't have cared less.

Galal was an Arab nationalist; he wished to see the colonial powers defeated in the war, if necessary with the aid of the Nazis. While Helmy and the other Berlin Egyptians were languishing in detention in 1939, Galal had taken advantage of the fact that his rival Riad Ahmed Mohamed—the politically moderate leader of the Islam Institute—was among their number. Riad Ahmed Mohamed had been leader of many other associations besides, including the Islamic community and the German-Muslim Society, and he favoured a comparatively pro-British, non-militant brand of anti-colonialism.

In November 1939, Galal had seized this opportunity to stage a coup against his compatriots, bringing about a complete change of leadership at the Berlin Islam Institute and appointing himself as its new General Secretary.[12] In this way, he had acceded to the centre of Muslim power in Berlin, such as it was. When the Grand Mufti arrived in 1941 with his extensive entourage, he needed someone to advise him on the local customs and practices,[13] and the SS and Foreign Office had turned to Galal as a trusted ally.

At the same time, Helmy and Galal could well remember the time during their student days when the Berlin imam had used his first article in the *Moslemische Revue* to castigate anti-Semitism as a crude Christian aberration. 'Jews have always been persecuted by Christians', the imam had lamented in 1924. 'Time and time again, the world has seen the bitter consequences of national hatred and religious prejudice. The world war has paralysed the whole of Europe and plunged it into hardship and misery. The nations should therefore learn their lesson at last and seek every available means to prevent the reoccurrence of such a calamity. They should avoid anything that generates hatred. Accordingly, each should recognize the other's religion. We should honour those things which the religions have in common.'[14]

Although Galal spent his days working dutifully for the Grand Mufti, he would occasionally let his guard down when his boss held forth on matters such as the depiction of the Jewish character in the Quran. In listing all the attributes of the Jews, the Grand Mufti declared, it 'burdens them with the eternal curse and condemns them to never make good because they carry the divine curse. This divine curse is expressed in the ignoble character of the Jews and their propensity for evil.'[15]

On one occasion, the SS chief Himmler, clearly impressed by such speeches, asked for someone to scan the Quran for passages that could be interpreted as evidence that Hitler's coming had been preordained in order to complete the Prophet's work.[16] Galal was duly approached, but declined. For heaven's sake, how stupid did they think Berlin's Muslims were?

Another Nazi leader would not take no for an answer, however. The Reich Security Head Office chief Ernst Kaltenbrunner claimed to know better. Hitler, he pontificated, had all the characteristics of Isa (Jesus), the prophet predicted in the Quran to return and inflict a St George-style defeat on Dajjal, the giant King of the Jews[17]—a figure who is, incidentally, nowhere to be found in the Quran itself.

The SS planned to have a million pamphlets printed, in the expectation that they would have a 'favourable effect' on the attitude of Muslims in south-eastern Europe, as well as reinforcing anti-Semitic tendencies in Palestine. Galal could only shake his head at the 'few incoherent sentences which, in my view, are only fit for the wastepaper basket'. Nor did he make any attempt to conceal his opinion from the propaganda ministry. 'I'm afraid that's all I can say on this matter', he wrote to Goebbels's people.[18]

Undeterred by Galal's practical objections, the SS went ahead and printed a million of the pocket-sized pamphlets. 'O Arabs, do you see that the time of the Dajjal has come? Do you recognize him, the fat, curly-haired Jew who deceives and rules the whole world and who steals the land of the Arabs?...O Arabs, do you know the servant of God? He has already appeared in the world and already turned his lance against the Dajjal and his allies.'[19] Galal could only look on in disbelief.

He knew, of course, how popular Islam had become with the Nazi regime. And just like Helmy, he saw in it a chance of survival. In their eagerness to ingratiate themselves with Muslims, high-ranking Nazi leaders were increasingly working themselves up into a bizarre veneration of Islam. In his memoirs, Albert Speer cites one of Hitler's infamous monologues, which he summarizes thus: 'When the Mohammedans attempted to penetrate beyond France into Central Europe during the eighth century, they had been driven back at the Battle of Tours. Had the Arabs won this battle, the world would be Mohammedan today #x2019; This notion of the so-called Islamization of the West was attractive to the Führer: 'For theirs was a religion that believed in spreading the faith by the sword and subjugating all nations to that faith. The Germanic peoples would have become heirs to that religion. Such a creed was perfectly suited to the Germanic temperament. Hitler said that the conquering Arabs, because of their racial inferiority, would in the long run have been unable to contend with the harsher climate and conditions of the country. They could not have kept down the more vigorous native, so that ultimately not

Arabs but Islamized Germans could have stood at the head of this Mohammedan Empire.'

Holed up in his bunker under a Berlin already in flames, Hitler would end this discourse with the observation: 'You see, it's been our misfortune to have the wrong religion…The Mohammedan religion would have been much more compatible to us than Christianity. Why did it have to be Christianity with its meekness and flabbiness?'[20]

At the same time, Galal had long realized what a transparent charade this was on the part of the Nazis, and how insincere their much-vaunted attachment to Islam was in reality. He had seen for himself that the Nazi ideologues had only taken this tone after a series of propaganda manoeuvres. Imams praying for Hitler, religious invocations out of the mouths of NS officers: the Nazis certainly saw a strategic opportunity here to appeal to religious sentiments. But they were flexible. At the Party's Christmas celebration in Munich back in 1925, Hitler had declared National Socialism to be nothing short of a 'practical fulfilment of the teachings of Christ'.[21]

In a speech at the Circus Krone in the early 1920s, before an audience of lower-middle-class Catholics, uprooted soldiers, and displaced academics, the Nazi demagogue had even compared himself to Jesus: 'We may be small, but another man once stood up in Galilee, and today his teachings dominate the whole world.' And in a letter of 1921 to Bavaria's conservative First Minister Gustav Ritter von Kahr, the Nazi propagandist Rudolf Hess wrote that Hitler was 'a character of rare decency and sincerity, generous in heart and religious, a good Catholic'.[22] Was this all an act? Undoubtedly—just like his suddenly discovered reverence for Islam.

In order to realize the fiercely anti-Semitic version of Islam they envisaged, it seemed that the Nazis first had to cultivate it with the aid of the Grand Mufti. The place they chose for this was Dresden. Through the net curtains of a villa in the elegant district of Blasewitz, a 'mysterious Mohammedan work party' could occasionally be seen meeting,[23] according to the underground diary of Victor Klemperer, brother of the Jewish medical professor Georg Klemperer who had once been Helmy's boss at the hospital. The property was now empty, having originally belonged to a Jewish family before being commandeered as a *Judenhaus*, where Jews were concentrated before being sent to their deaths.

SS officers carried vases into the building, followed by mosaics of Central Asian design and tiles bearing verses from the Quran.[24] All this activity was part of a secret project: the establishment of an SS mullah school. Under the aegis of the Grand Mufti, several dozen Muslim clerics—the pro-Nazi whippers-in of tomorrow—were trained here.

Muslim Berlin had been a melting pot. Happily for Anna and 'Nadia', a world of fluid boundaries had emerged where Rolf morphed into Mohamed and Ingeborg into Amina, and where first names or surnames could be double-barrelled. Helmy and Galal were well aware of this, and found fertile ground for the deliberate confusion they planned to sow with Anna's new identity.

In the 1920s, many people had come to the mosque to search for meaning. As the French-Jewish satirist Yvan Goll quipped, 'Happy were the insane, all those who resorted to the classics, phenomenology, numismatics, Taoism, or any of the myriad sects with patents on God.'[25] Consequently, a third of Berlin's Muslims were converts. It would have required a miracle to maintain an overview of all this. In Goll's words, 'A few handfuls of Buddhist rice, three teaspoons of Christian holy water, a little Muslim rose oil, a clove of Jewish garlic plus a pinch of Platonic salt made a cake that tasted better than the daily army bread that came wrapped up in some hawkish newspaper article.'[26]

For a while, the Wilmersdorf mosque had even promoted itself by advertising how easy it was to convert. 'No formal ceremony is necessary in order to become a Muslim. Islam is not just a rational, widespread, and practically applicable religion, but is also fully in tune with natural human tendencies. Every child is born with these tendencies. Therefore, no one has to undergo a conversion in order to become a Muslim. One can be a Muslim without telling anyone. Professing one's faith in Islam is simply a formality for organizational purposes.'[27]

Even though the Nazis had since tried to erect new barriers with their race laws—barriers so hard and fast that Jews at least would no longer be able to escape them—Anna still retained the hope that a person's tracks could disappear in the general muddle.

'Berlin, 10 June 1943', Galal began tapping on the typewriter. It was a Thursday. A starry night with no clouds and no air raid warnings. At the top of the piece of paper documenting Anna's supposed religious conversion, Galal typed 'To Whom It May Concern'. In the letterhead stood the name of the Grand Mufti. 'This is to certify that Miss Annie Boros has converted to the Islamic religion and is now consequently a Muslim.'[28] Underneath, Galal signed his own name.

And so it was that, on that June night, the fictional character Nadia acquired her first official documentation.

# A PAPER MARRIAGE

A whole network of Arab friends and confidants were engaged in helping Helmy to protect Anna. They never ceased to wonder, however, at the assortment of characters to whom Helmy entrusted his sensitive secret. First it had been the propaganda writer Galal, who worked for the Nazis alongside the stridently anti-Semitic Grand Mufti and the hate-spewing Goebbels. This time, it seemed, the individual in question was a jazz musician with a penchant for clarinets and crepe dresses.

It was pitch-black when Anna and the musician met at Helmy's apartment. The date was 16 June 1943, just a week after Anna's conversion to Islam, and Helmy had chosen it in order to execute stage two of his plan to procure Anna a legal route out of Berlin: a paper marriage, or *mariage blanc*, as they called it in Egypt.[1] First the conversion to Islam, and now marriage to a Muslim. 'Nadia' was gradually transitioning from fiction to reality.

The door of the apartment opened a crack. Light spilled into the hallway, and in came Abdel Aziz Helmy Hammad. He was thirty-six, five years younger than Helmy. The two of them had met in Gestapo detention in 1939, where they had become friends.

Three years into the war, Hammad still lived in style: describing a typical Friday night, he said he had been out with two friends from Vienna, a Mr Barth and a Miss Milla. Sometime after ten, the three of them had gone to the Uhu bar in the Lutherstraße, where they 'sat down together at a table and drank six bottles of Sekt'.[2]

The musician's circumstances had clearly not been reduced by the war, Anna observed, as he talked, eyes half-closed, of the Mampe herb liqueur and Mumm Sekt that continued to flow inexhaustibly in Hitler's capital. As a foreign visitor to the city had once sneered, 'Sodom and Gomorrah were alive and well in Berlin'.[3]

Two witnesses now also stepped out of the darkness into the bright apartment, much to Anna's bewilderment. She looked at Helmy. Was it really necessary to let any more of his Arab friends into the secret?

But without witnesses it wouldn't have been a valid sharia marriage, Helmy had replied—in which case there would have been no point in even trying the new plan.

One of the witnesses was Mohamed Sulaiman as-Safar, a friend in Berlin. The other was Riad Ahmed Mohamed—the very same Egyptian who had been ousted and robbed of political power by the Arab nationalist Kamal el-Din Galal while in Gestapo custody in 1939. Helmy, it appeared, was friends with both: the enemy of the British and their ally. It is remarkable, given their vastly different and indeed mutually hostile attitudes, that both were willing to assist him in protecting a Jew. They too were part of the ever-growing network that Helmy was secretly cultivating while keeping up the pretence of absolute loyalty to the Party.

The idea had come to Helmy some time ago, in November 1942.[4] Back then, he had asked Anna to find out whether the Romanian Consulate would object if she lost her Romanian passport and gained an Egyptian one through marriage. The official reply gave him grounds for hope: 'We would advise that, if the

**Fig. 8.** Egypt was a place of longing for Jews during World War II

marriage is approved by the Egyptian authorities and solemnized here, Miss Boros would—as far as we are aware—thereby acquire Egyptian citizenship.'[5]

Helmy had already made several attempts to obtain an Egyptian passport for Anna, which would have enabled her to get to Egypt and thence to Palestine. He had tried to adopt her, but his application was refused.[6] All efforts to get Anna out of the country were 'thwarted by insurmountable difficulties', Helmy later recalled.[7] Perhaps, just as things were getting desperate, he had chanced to hear the story of Risa Wortsmann.

Risa Wortsmann was a Jewish girl from Vienna who had turned up in Berlin in 1938. She was seventeen at the time, the same age that Anna was now. Risa had met a handsome young Egyptian chemistry student at a Viennese night club; he was known as Harry, though his real name was Hussein. The couple had come to

Berlin to have their marriage recognized. It was a nerve-racking time: they had to submit their papers to the Egyptian Consulate and wait to see if the diplomats would approve them. In Risa's case, the attempt was successful: she acquired Harry's Egyptian nationality, which allowed her to emigrate to London. Not only that, but her whole family were able to follow her.[8]

Back in Helmy's apartment, the doctor seated himself on the floor. He would speak for Anna, in the role of what the Egyptians called a *Maasun*, meaning an older representative who led the marriage ceremony and spoke on behalf of the bride. Anna was to remain silent throughout. The two witnesses sat likewise.

'Sharia Marriage', Helmy wrote on a piece of paper. It had to be a religious ceremony—there was no other way. Only then would Anna have any hope of avoiding a trip to the registry office where, at the latest, her cover would have been blown. Her conversion to Islam a few days previously was evidently just a precondition for this ceremony: a religious act of which the authorities would be notified after the event, in the hope that they would ask as few questions as possible.

Perhaps Helmy had already heard of the sham marriage networks that extended as far as Egypt. The Jewish hospital in Alexandria in particular had become a hub for such activities. There, an enterprising nurse named Thea Wolf, from the German city of Essen, bribed the Egyptian port police by offering them free circumcisions for their sons. Thus appeased, they refrained from arresting illegal Jewish boat refugees from Europe and allowed them to come to her instead. The nurse then went about finding Egyptians willing to enter into a *mariage blanc*. Her clients paid fifty Egyptian pounds for the wedding and a further fifty on divorce. The trick worked, saving many lives. Some of the Jewish women naturalized in this way 'even managed to ask their parents over to visit them in Egypt', Wolf later wrote in her memoirs. 'They duly came, and so escaped the Holocaust in the land of the Eternal Nile.'[9] It was a plan of this kind that Helmy and his co-conspirators had in mind for Anna.

Helmy took up his pen and began to write in somewhat stilted Arabic: 'On this evening of Wednesday, 16 June 1943, the marriage has taken place of Mr Abdel Aziz Helmy Hammad, having reached his thirty-sixth year and being born on 6 May 1906 in Fakous in the Province of Sharqiya and currently resident at Johann-Georg-Straße 23 in the city of Berlin. The marriage was concluded with Miss Nadia Boros, being a Muslim, born on 22 November 1925 in Arad in the state of Romania, a Romanian citizen and resident at Neue Friedrichstraße 77 in the city of Berlin.'[10]

The bridegroom was not only a jazz musician, but also a long-standing and courageous opponent of the Nazis, and so Helmy had every reason to trust him, above all others, with this risky project. Hammad was someone who had long continued to defend the Jewish–Islamic symbiosis of the 1920s against the Nazis. To the west of the Kaiser Wilhelm Memorial Church on the Kurfürstendamm, there were a dozen or so bars concentrated within a space of perhaps five thousand square metres: the Königin, the Roxy, the Uhu, the Kakadu, the Rosita, and the Patria,[11] and in the midst of them all was the Oriental restaurant Shark (meaning 'East') at Uhlandstraße 20/21.[12] Hammad himself was the manager of the Carlton bar on Rankestraße, a small side street off the Kurfürstendamm.

Here, liveried porters chased away all but the most elegant and distinguished-looking visitors, a policy which also tended to keep out the detested spies of the Reich Chamber of Music (RMK), who were always shabbily dressed. On the rare occasions that they did manage to force their way in, on the lookout for Jewish musicians or anyone playing the 'nigger' or 'Jewish' jazz of Irving Berlin or George Gershwin, the artists on the stage would be warned in advance by a secret bell, and would display sham song titles on their sheet music. 'Tiger Rag' would be exchanged for something suitably anodyne, like the swing band hit 'Schwarzer Panther',[13] and the Nazi censors would be none the wiser.

By the time the Gestapo interned him along with Helmy in 1939, Anna's bridegroom had already been shunting Jewish musicians around for years. Thanks to him, the Jewish violinist Paul Weinapel, who had lost his engagement in the late 1930s under pressure from the RMK, was able to move his band from the Sherbini to the Ciro bar. While the RMK were otherwise occupied, he was then quietly re-engaged at the Sherbini.[14]

The Ciro was directly adjacent to Hammad's Carlton bar, and it too was run by an Egyptian, Ahmed Mustafa. He had come to Berlin in the late 1920s and enjoyed initial success as a vaudeville dancer before pulling in the late-night crowds with artists such as the swing pianist Fritz Schulz-Reichel, otherwise known as 'Crazy Otto', famous for pressing thumbtacks into the felt of his piano hammers to create the typical turn-of-the-century barrelhouse sound.[15]

The Ciro's bright terracotta walls were hung with kitsch paintings on Egyptian themes, from Cleopatra to King Farouk. 'Up a few more stairs, we find ourselves in the silver room, from where we can let the elegant nightlife wash over us', one visitor marvelled.[16] The only venue more elegant than this one was the aforementioned Sherbini, run by another Egyptian, Mostafa el-Sherbini—a good-looking dandy and jazz percussionist who had married the stepdaughter of a count.[17] All these people were part of Hammad's network.

The time had come to present the *mahar*, the gift from groom to bride. Dr Helmy, as *Maasun*, settled on a symbolic sum of a hundred marks. Picking up the pen again, he concluded his text with the words: 'This marriage is recognized religiously according to the Book of God and the commandments of His Prophet.'[18]

Finally, he invited all those present to sign, and Anna took the pen and wrote her Muslim name squarely on the paper—*Nadia*.

# THE GESTAPO CLOSES IN

In the mornings, when the Spree was still exhaling its cool, musty night breath, Anna would sometimes go down to the waterside with Emmy. The two young women had taken to each other well. They would walk the dog and take their time, like two ordinary relatives or friends, before beginning their working day at the practice. If anyone addressed them, Emmy, the elder of the two, would reply. The girl was a niece of her Arab fiancé; such a well-brought-up child. For her part, Anna would nod pleasantly and say nothing.[1]

When the letter from the Charlottenburg registry office arrived, a week after Anna's nocturnal sharia marriage to Hammad, she opened it cautiously, like a precious object. The letter said the case had been examined, but the marriage could 'not take place'. The plan to procure Anna an Egyptian passport—and hence a ticket to freedom—by marrying her into the small community of Berlin Muslims had 'failed due to the opposition of the German authorities', as Anna later reported.[2] If she hadn't already felt as if the rug had been pulled from under her feet, then the last sentence of the stark missive was probably the last straw: 'You are requested to collect the submitted certificates from our office at the earliest opportunity.'[3]

This was a trap; her escape route was blocked. What alarmed Anna most, however, was the reason given by the registry office for its decision.

The Nazi racial policies required a racial test to be performed prior to any marriage between a 'Hamite' and a German.[4] Helmy and Emmy had already hit the same obstacle themselves: shortly before Christmas 1939, they had announced their engagement and attempted to marry, only to be prevented on grounds of 'race', as Helmy later explained.[5] Not that this word was ever used in the authorities' official declarations. The bureaucratic euphemism was 'capacity to contract marriage'.

And now Anna and Hammad were facing a similar rejection from the Charlottenburg registry office: 'The Minister of Justice is not in a position to grant you the requested exemption from the obligation to produce a certificate of no impediment to marriage.'[6] This was worrying news. Indeed, it set alarm bells ringing, as nowhere in the submitted marriage documents had Anna's secret been disclosed, or any mention been made of her Jewishness. Rather, she was referred to exclusively as 'Miss Nadia', who was identified explicitly as a Muslim. To all appearances, therefore, the marriage was a purely inter-Muslim one. Surely that would have been acceptable even to the Nazi race guardians? And yet the authorities were clearly treating this sharia arrangement as a mixed marriage, not a purely Muslim one, as if they sensed that something was wrong.

Shortly after the letter of rejection from the registry office at the end of June 1943 came an even more alarming communication: Anna was required to report to the Romanian Consulate as soon as possible in preparation for 'emigration'.[7] It was a year since she had last received a summons of this kind, and she had assumed the matter long since closed. At that time, Anna's parents had managed to shake off the Gestapo by claiming that she had emigrated to Romania at her own initiative.

The latest letter had been sent to Anna's old address in the Neue Friedrichstraße, the long-since 'Aryanized' apartment above the greengrocer's—now deserted save for occasional visits by her grandmother's steward, Otto Buja, to pick up the mail. The authorities had evidently put two and two together. Helmy had written the old address of the real Anna on 'Nadia's' sharia marriage certificate: a careless mistake.

As a result of the marriage application, the Gestapo were now also back on Anna's trail, as Anna and Helmy must have realized by now. By signing the sharia documents, Helmy had made himself a target for the authorities. He had vouched for 'Nadia' in his role as *Maasun*. Where, once they were ready to strike, would the Gestapo snoopers search, if not at his place? What would they do to him, now that he had made such fools of them?

Just as Anna received these chilling letters, more trucks were rolling through Moabit carrying terrified people from the nearby freight depot. On 28 June 1943, a load of 314 deportees left Moabit bound for Auschwitz.

Reflecting after the war on this period in summer 1943, Helmy remembered feeling a growing sense of desperation: 'The Gestapo repeatedly approached the caretaker of Krefelder Straße 7 inquiring about me and the hidden Jewish girl. Twice they carried out a search of my apartment and asked questions.'[8] As Anna recalled, 'The doctor had to find me somewhere else to live and a food supply.'[9]

At Helmy's, they were a sitting target. Nine tenants of Krefelder Straße 7 had already descended the staircase for the last time in

1941, 1942, and 1943, some on their own two feet, some dragged by the Gestapo. The two Conitzer daughters next door were not much older than Anna. The elder of the two, Ursula, had married and fled with her husband to Palestine in 1938. The younger one, Ruth, failed to escape in time, having only made it as far as Gut Winkel, near Fürstenwalde, an agricultural training college designed to prepare Jews for emigration to Palestine. She was murdered at Auschwitz on 1 March 1943, and her parents, Helmy's next-door neighbours, on 12 January 1943. Only the Lessers on the ground floor—the tobacconist and his wife—would eventually come out of Theresienstadt alive.[10]

Henceforward, all that protected Anna from suspicious neighbours and the Gestapo was the thin veil of her Muslim disguise. And the game of hide-and-seek became even more precarious when her mother suddenly turned up on the doorstep, wearing the yellow badge on her coat.

# THE FINAL LIE

As an illegal, Anna had to get by without the yellow, green, blue, red, and pink ration cards. For as long as they could, her mother and stepfather continued to bring her a few provisions.[1] The only time when Anna's real family could get together in 1943 was on Sunday afternoons, behind closed curtains at Helmy's apartment. This was also the only place where they could obtain news of Anna's grandmother, whose sole channel of communication was her former office manager, Otto Buja.[2] Helmy's home was the epicentre of it all.

Would it not have been safer to receive these troublesome guests by night? Helmy thought differently: better to visit by day, then the neighbours would be less suspicious. After all, he reasoned, what was so unusual about a doctor receiving visits from former patients?

But Anna was annoyed. Whenever her mother and 'Fatty', her stepfather, came to dinner on a Sunday, she later reflected, 'they talked of nothing but Jews and displaced people'.[3] Never a word about the danger facing their hosts, the ostensibly German-Muslim household of Helmy, Emmy, and 'Nadia'. Anna's mother and stepfather were in a much less vulnerable position. Her stepfather wasn't Jewish, and her mother had so far been protected from deportation by her marriage. They could live their life in the open, as legal citizens, and incautious behaviour on their part was much more likely to endanger Anna and Helmy than themselves.

After a spell of forced labour at the raw material wholesalers Rose & Co. in the Schöneberg district, Anna's mother now worked as a shop clerk at Herrmann's in the neighbourhood of Prenzlauer Berg.[4] Anna's stepfather, Georg Wehr, was likewise still at liberty, having avoided conscription. Although married to a Jew, he benefited from the fact that the sausage factory he currently worked for supplied the army and was therefore considered essential to the war effort.[5]

One Sunday evening when the family was gathered at Helmy's, there was a sudden knock at the door. Outside was a young man, his face bloodied and bruised. It was Anna's half-uncle, Martin Rudnik. The Gestapo had beaten him so badly that he would remain hard of hearing in his left ear for the rest of his life.[6] He was still living at Hildegard Ullbrich's in Wilmersdorf, where he made money through black-marketeering. It was almost impossible for him to avoid being seen now and again by other tenants, especially when there were air raid warnings. This wasn't the first time that someone—relishing their own sense of power—had denounced him. But it had never been as bad as this before.

The first time, he had been lucky under the circumstances. He had been taken by the local police to the Gestapo headquarters in the Burgstraße, for transferral to the assembly camp in the Levetzowstraße. Fortunately for him, however, he was to be escorted there by Jewish security guards, one of whom he knew. It was dark, and when they reached the Victory Column he had managed to jump from the truck and return on foot to Wilmersdorf.[7]

This time, it had been a different story. A former employee of the company Hrabowski, which had an office on the

Alexanderplatz in the same building as the family's greengrocery, had recognized Martin in the street and denounced him. Once again, he was taken to the Burgstraße, and this time subjected to horrific abuse. The Gestapo officers had tried to extract the name of his protector from him under torture, but Martin had stood firm and refused to betray Hildegard Ullbrich. Once at the assembly camp, he had managed miraculously to escape through a window. After that, he knew he couldn't go straight back to his protector without putting her life in danger.[8]

Therefore, instead of running to Hildegard's, Martin had decided to burden Helmy with the risk and join the family for Sunday dinner at his place. He stood in the doorway fighting for breath, until Helmy pulled him quickly inside. Anna was aghast: 'You can imagine how dangerous this was for the doctor', she later reflected.[9]

But Helmy showed no sign of anger; on the contrary, he lent Martin money and saw that he was fed and watered. Only then did the young man move on to other acquaintances.[10]

Anna could see that her own family was becoming an increasing source of danger to Helmy. For his part, Helmy endeavoured to put new precautions in place, and hastened to find a new emergency hiding place for Anna. As a brief stopgap, he managed to place her with his patient Frieda Szturmann in Staaken, who already had her hands full with Anna's grandmother Cecilie. From there, she moved on to Frieda's sister in Lichterfelde, and then to a nurse named Schmidt in Neukölln.[11] 'After three weeks', Anna reports, 'the doctor ventured to take me in again.'[12]

More importantly, however, Dr Helmy came up with a new, even bigger lie in order to mask the many small ones he had already told the Gestapo for Anna's sake. This one was for emergencies, and took the form of a self-addressed letter which he dictated to Anna. That done, he folded it up and put it in his pocket.

Anna's lungs were making rattling noises. She had frostbite on both legs.[13] It was horribly cold among the bare birch trees of Berlin-Buch, an estate on the northern edge of the city's Pankow district. The cabins were covered with nothing but tar paper; moss sprouted from the gaps between the boards. Since the nights had come to be dominated by the wailing of sirens and the flash of bombs, more and more people were moving out into shelters like these. The longer the war wore on, and the stronger the sense that the country was back where it started, the bigger this exodus became. Jews were also among those who took refuge in community gardens. Hans Rosenthal, later to become a famous German quiz show host, was a teenager like Anna when he went into hiding in the garden colony 'Dreieinigkeit' in Lichtenberg, and Julius Meysel, father of the popular German actress Inge Meysel, was in his early fifties when he hid in his secretary's riverside summerhouse in Köpenick.

The regime threatened repeatedly to send in the building inspectors in order to check that no one was living illegally in garden colonies; the warning 'could not be stated often enough', as the Nazi newspaper *Völkischer Beobachter* declared belligerently. In reality, however, the last inspection had been carried out three years since, and it was now late 1943. Moreover, the wildly inconsistent figures obtained by the authorities showed how utterly they had lost the overview. Were there now 120,000 'permanent lodgers' in Berlin's community gardens, or 2,500, or 49,000?[14] All this chaos offered a degree of protection, as Helmy realized.

Having installed Anna in the cabin in Berlin-Buch, Helmy and Emmy came out to join her following the partial destruction of their apartment building in Moabit in an air raid on 27 November 1943.[15] Helmy had succeeded in keeping the existence of the place secret from the Gestapo.[16] 'He managed to evade all the Gestapo's interrogations', Anna recalled.[17] Perhaps he had rented the plot at Hörstenweg 70 under a false name. Perhaps it didn't belong to him at all, but to Emmy's family.

The girl's presence drew suspicious glances at the community garden. Some people smelt a rat. Anna couldn't bank on being safe from exposure for very long, but had no other choice than to continue playing her role. 'My daughter couldn't just sit around,' Anna's mother related, 'otherwise she would have been found out. She was simply too young. The doctor took her with him every day to the practice in Berlin, despite the serious risks involved.'[18]

Anna continued to don her headscarf every morning, and Helmy continued to take her with him to Charlottenburg every day. They had weighed up the pros and cons and concluded that a sudden interruption of their routine would be even riskier, as it would have attracted attention and led to questions. Instead, they opted to go on with the show.

Cautious as they were, however, the biggest hazard lay closer to home. It wasn't a curious neighbour or a sharp-eyed block warden they needed to worry about: it was Anna's mother. Though still enjoying legal status and remaining safe from deportation, she nevertheless had to report for forced labour every morning. In this way, as Anna learnt to her horror, Julie's workmates 'gradually got to know the whole story of me and my hiding place'.[19]

Perhaps the tale of the Jewish girl disguised as a Muslim was simply too irresistible for Julie to keep it entirely to herself. Anna had feared as much: her mother's constant quest for recognition made it difficult for her to control herself. 'Even though we urged her daily not to tell anyone', Anna lamented, Julie 'never learned'. She was appalled by her mother's recklessness and her 'complete lack of self-restraint', as she commented after the war.[20]

And so it was that the Gestapo discovered the subterfuge and duly took action. Anna's mother was arrested on 10 January 1945. The officers took her for further questioning at the assembly camp at Schulstraße 78—the former pathology building of the Jewish hospital which had since replaced the camp in the Große Hamburger Straße.[21] The Gestapo wanted to know the whereabouts of her phoney Muslim daughter. Everyone had heard about their torture methods, and no one knew whether they would be able to hold out against them. That was when Julie, as she later admitted, 'made the mistake of giving away my daughter's location'.[22]

'Those were terrible days and nights', Anna later recalled.[23] Finally, it was time for Helmy to enact his emergency plan. His first step was to go straight to the state police department in the Burgstraße seeking an interview with the Gestapo. Nothing betrays a person more than a guilty conscience, he reasoned. But perhaps a brisk air of overwhelming self-conviction would do the trick. Helmy had had plenty of practice at this, so much so that he had become a master of the art. He sought out the very officers who were engaged in the hunt for Anna and told them with a look of practised innocence: I am the victim of a deception. Worse still, he added, raising his voice to a pitch of indignant accusation: a Jewish girl has tricked her way into my home!

**Fig. 9.** 'Those were terrible days and nights', Anna recalled. Bombs would light up the night sky amid the wailing of sirens

What Helmy did next was his final tour de force. He produced the letter he had dictated to Anna from his pocket. This last fantasy, he hoped, would cover up all the others.

In the letter, Anna confessed ruefully that she had 'lied to him about her ancestry', and was in reality Jewish. She was writing this letter to tell the doctor that she had decided to leave him and go to her aunt's in Dessau.[24]

Helmy explained that he had discovered the letter after the girl had disappeared without trace. Far from being in on the conspiracy, he had found himself duped by her.

How could Helmy expect the Gestapo officers to swallow such a transparent lie? That he had taken in a strange girl with no papers, yet never suspected that she might be a Jew? Would anyone really buy his story? Surely it was beyond the bounds of credibility that this Jewish girl could have persuaded Helmy—an Arab and a Muslim—that she too was not only both of those things but also a relative? And, even more improbably, that she had happened to go underground, bound for Dessau, on the very day that the Gestapo had learned of her secret refuge at Helmy's?

Gentlemen, Helmy urged them with the utmost gravity, you must find this witch! And with that, he held his breath.

# VISIT TO CAIRO

The rubbish has evidently been accumulating for some time in front of the wooden gate. A small, sinewy tabby cat paws at a knotted plastic bag until mandarin peel bursts out of it, followed by a collection of nappies, twigs, and cigarette stubs. All around, the ground-floor windows are sealed with bars and wire netting to prevent passers-by from throwing in junk and stones, as is already the case on the first floor, where the jagged edges of broken panes are covered in soot.

If you go to Cairo today and look up from this gate, which stands at the end of a long, dusty market street, you will see two white marble tablets. Inscribed on them are the Ten Commandments. *Anochi Adonai*—I am the Lord, your God. *Lo Tirzach*—Thou shalt not kill. The Hebrew text was skilfully chiselled into the stone a long time ago; underneath it, a more recent hand has scribbled a few obscene words in Arabic with a marker pen.

This is the only synagogue left in Cairo's former Jewish quarter, where there were once fifteen. Small Suzuki vans laden with boxes squeeze through a lane barely three metres across. The market streets of this city are organized thematically: this one specializes in girls' toys—glittery trinkets, bracelets, cuddly toys. Once, the Jewish quarter encompassed three hundred such streets; today, the name of this one—Haret al-Yahud or 'Jewish Alley'—is the sole relic of Jewish life in the El-Gamaleya district, the 'place of the beautiful'. The tabby picks at a gnawed corn cob and is shooed away. It is a good hundred years since Mohamed Helmy lived here, in Egypt's capital, with its large Jewish minority.

Today, it is no longer possible to hear the story of Helmy and Anna first-hand. Anna died in New York in 1986, Helmy in Berlin in 1982. But it is still told by people like Professor Nasser Kotby, a relative of Helmy living in Cairo. It is well worth the trip to see him, as well as other members of Helmy's large family. In their mouths, however, it is no longer just a story of the past, but also one of the present.

When the synagogue in Haret al-Yahud was consecrated in 1910, it was named after perhaps the greatest medieval Jewish thinker, Moses Maimonides. Or rather 'Ibn Maimun', as Professor Kotby corrects with a smile. 'Let's put the record straight: he wasn't called Maimonides. Maimonides is the Grecianized version. His real name was Ibn Maimun.'

The broad-shouldered, white-haired man cuts an elegant figure in his pinstriped suit. The sun is beating down, and he seeks shade in front of the decaying synagogue. He is a great-nephew of Helmy—an eighty-year-old retired professor of medicine at Egypt's second-largest university.

According to Professor Kotby, Ibn Maimun, the universal scholar of the medieval period, was a man all Egyptians should be proud of. As indeed they should of many Jews: of Leila Mourad, the superstar of the Arabic chanson and Egypt's most popular female singer in Helmy's youth; and of numerous other artists, composers, and thinkers besides. Before the war, the professor reflects, Egypt had been a land of three religions. There were Christian ministers and Jewish ones. The Jews were part of society.

Moses Maimonides, or Ibn Maimun, argued as far back as the Middle Ages for an allegorical rather than a literal interpretation of the Bible—a fact much trumpeted by philosophers of the nineteenth-century Jewish Enlightenment. One of his axioms was: 'The inability of our reason, which prevents us from understanding [God's] Essence, is like the inability of our eyes to gaze on the light of the sun', except that his original reference was to 'Allah' rather than God. He wrote nearly all his texts in his native Arabic, and lived in Cairo.

A hundred years ago, when Mohamed Helmy was a schoolboy, there were still around 150,000 Egyptian Jews living in the country. According to Professor Kotby, a cousin of Helmy's had been married to a Jewish woman who ran an haute couture business in Cairo. Then the bloody pogroms against Egypt's Jewish minority began in 1945, culminating in a series of bombings in 1949. Arab nationalists declared their Jewish neighbours enemy aliens. Smoke rose from the streets of El-Gamaleya, and cries rang out at night. By 1956, nearly all Egyptian Jews had been driven from their homeland. Today, there are said to be just a hundred left in the whole country.

Nowadays, Professor Kotby frowns, 'malicious tongues would have you believe that Egypt is full of Jews'. As he explains, however, this is just a form of backbiting. In Egypt, he says, claiming that someone is of Jewish origin or has a Jewish wife has become a common way of discrediting them. 'We were educated from childhood that the Holocaust is a big lie', Muhammad al-Zurquani, editor-in-chief of the Egyptian state newspaper *Al-Liwaa Al-Islami*,

**Fig. 10.** Star of David and crescent moon: the synagogue gate in Cairo unites the two symbols, but the building now stands in ruins

wrote in 2004 in an article entitled 'The Lie about the Burning of the Jews'. In the eyes of a large part of the population, the genocide of the European Jews is purely a Zionist invention.

Although the Ibn Maimun synagogue is now a ruin, another Jewish house of prayer still remains in use in Cairo. Shar Hashamayim—Hebrew for 'Gate of Heaven'—can be found in Adly Street, a wide, busy road. From the outside, the place has a bunker-like appearance, standing twenty-five metres tall, with two rows of small barred windows interspersed with stylized palms bearing plump coconuts and Stars of David. Even on Saturday mornings, the time of the Shabbat morning service, it always looks deserted. The building is patrolled by Egyptian police with automatic pistols, ready to turn away any curious visitor unfamiliar with the hidden rear entrances.

Professor Kotby prefers to remember a past when Jews could move around more freely in this country. 'They were almost always persecuted in Europe, whereas in the Middle East—among a Muslim majority—they lived in peace.' Were those more tolerant times? 'No', he replies. 'It's not about tolerance! That's tantamount to saying I can put up with the fact that you see things differently from me, but I wouldn't care if you disappeared off the face of the earth. I would be neither better nor worse off for it. "Tolerance" is not a good word. It's about mutual esteem.'

The professor often went to Berlin after the war to visit his great-uncle Helmy. They would go to the theatre or to a restaurant, and sometimes they would 'visit my grandmother', as he puts it. 'She used to live in Charlottenburg. Now she lives on an island.' He is referring to the famous statuette of Queen Nefertiti on Museum Island.

Why Helmy was still living in Germany after the war is a question not even his Cairene relative can answer with any certainty. Didn't he ever want to get away from that bombed-out, impoverished, and deeply disgraced country? The professor shrugs, and talks about the good life that Helmy eventually came to enjoy there after the war. How he was finally allowed to marry his fiancée, Emmy. How the Allies, in search of politically untainted candidates, even put him in charge of Berlin-Buch Hospital.

Helmy was lucky. The gamble he took in spring 1945, when he presented the Gestapo with his last great cock-and-bull story, could have cost him his life. He had looked the Gestapo officers in the eye and staked everything on that one chance. They may well have had their suspicions. But—in the confusion of the final few weeks of war—it seems that no one bothered to check up on

Helmy's bizarre testimony. He could breathe a sigh of relief—and await the approaching end of the reign of terror.

On 21 April 1945, the Red Army reached Berlin-Buch.[1] Anna was able to discard the hijab and openly resume her true identity without having to fear for her life: the identity of a Jewish girl who owed her survival to Muslims.

A few years later, on 2 June 1960, at the offices of the New York notary Theodora W. Joven Hoyt, Anna raised her right hand, swore an affidavit and sent it both to the Jewish community in Berlin's Joachimstaler Straße and to the Mayor, requesting that an honour be conferred on Dr Helmy, a 'wonderful human being' who never wanted any thanks for what he did.

In autumn 2013, a medal was duly minted in Jerusalem bearing the words, 'Whosoever saves a single life saves an entire universe'—a Jewish maxim from the Talmud. Virtually the same words also appear in the Quran. To date, the Israeli Holocaust memorial centre Yad Vashem has recognized 25,000 brave men and women who rescued Jews during the Second World War as 'Righteous Among the Nations'. The most well known of these is the Frankfurt-born teenager Anne Frank, who was hidden from the Nazis in Amsterdam by the couple Miep and Jan Gies. The story related in this book is, however, unique. Although a hundred or so Muslims—mostly from the Balkans and Central Asia—have so far been recognized as Righteous, there is only one Arab: Helmy.

In due course, the doctor's relatives in Cairo received an invitation to Yad Vashem. It was to be quite an occasion. But they declined to go, being unwilling to accept the award because it came from Israel. The case briefly became politicized following a spate of comments on the Yad Vashem website insinuating the existence of a 'Zionist conspiracy' in which Helmy was the alleged 'useful idiot' of an Israeli propaganda stunt.

There is a history to this episode. The American historian Robert Satloff tried for years to tell the story of Arabs who saved the lives of their Jewish neighbours. Much of the research for his 2006 book *Among the Righteous* was done in North Africa, which was once home to large numbers of Jews. In 1940, France's Nazi-dependent Vichy regime introduced anti-Semitic laws in Morocco, but the Sultan, Mohamed V, refused to put them into practice; on the contrary, he demonstrated his opposition by inviting all the rabbis in the country to his Throne Day celebrations in Marrakesh.

To his astonishment, however, Satloff encountered a wall of resistance to his research into this subject: it was almost as if he had broken a taboo. He had expected the opposite to be the case, thinking that the Arab states would be glad to see the heroic deeds of their own citizens brought to public attention. 'I wrote diplomats and journalists, scholars and politicians,' Satloff reports, 'and the response was always the same—silence.'[2]

The researcher subsequently followed up a spectacular case in Paris—that of Si Kaddour Benghabrit, rector of the city's Grand Mosque, who is said to have hidden Jews during the Second World War. The story was brought vividly to life in the 2011 Cannes Film Festival winner *Free Men* by the French director Ismaël Ferroukhi. As Satloff discovered, however, it was more rooted in legend than reality.[3]

In 2007, he suggested that Yad Vashem extend the honour of 'Righteous Among the Nations' to the Tunisian Khaled Abdul-Wahab instead. But, to his further amazement, he was stonewalled again, this time by the director of the 'Righteous' department,

Irena Steinfeldt. She argued that the Tunisian didn't have to risk his own life—a precondition for awarding the title—when, in 1942, at the age of just thirty-one, he saved two Jewish families from deportation to the labour camps of the Nazi occupiers by sheltering them at his wealthy family's country residence.

A controversy ensued. Steinfeldt's predecessor, Mordecai Paldiel, pointed out that some Europeans had indeed been honoured merely on the basis of the 'risk of possible punishment', and that this was an opportunity to send out a signal to the Arab world.[4] But to no avail.

As the historian Satloff concludes, disputes of this kind are never just about the past, but invariably also about the present. For both groups—Jews and Arabs alike—the past is 'a powerful source of motivation, grievance, and legitimacy'.[5]

In Professor Kotby's living room there are dark wood hippopotamuses alongside Chinese lampions, Danish porcelain, and wood carvings from Oberammergau. Because it is Friday—the butler's day off—he serves the mallow tea himself. He has seen a great deal of the world and speaks many languages, but he too is opposed to the Jerusalem Holocaust memorial. 'Who made Yad Vashem the representative of all Jews?' he asks. At the time of Helmy's rescue activities in pre-1945 Berlin, he adds, there was no such thing as the state of Israel; even today, half of all Jews still live outside Israel. In his view, Yad Vashem is merely seeking to 'exploit Helmy's heroism for political purposes'.

Today, Dr Helmy's relatives live in Heliopolis, a quiet, leafy suburb of Cairo. There are hanging baskets outside, gold picture frames and embroidered cushions inside, and the French windows are open. It is dark by now, and two more relatives have arrived: ex-general Mohamed el-Kelish and ex-officer Ahmed Nur el-Din Farghal, a nephew and great-nephew of Helmy's respect-ively. They lean back in their heavy armchairs, sipping espresso between cigarettes. 'We would be delighted if another country honoured him. Helmy helped all people, no matter what their reli-gion. Now Israel wants to honour him specifically because he helped Jews. But this doesn't do justice to what he did.'

Nowadays, Jews and Muslims seem as far apart as they once were close, so profoundly has the past been eclipsed by more recent events, notably the conflict in the Middle East. Dr Helmy was a proud Muslim, says an elderly lady in a black hijab seated among the embroidered living room cushions. Mervat el-Kashab is the widow of another of Helmy's great-nephews. The ringtone on her smartphone is a call to prayer. 'It's completely irrelevant whether a person is Jewish, Muslim, or Christian', she insists. In her view, Helmy was driven by an instinct of humanity deeply rooted in Islam. 'We are all human beings.' It is a pity, she adds, that the state of Israel is the only country in the Middle East that takes a different view, by making such a clear distinction between Jews and Muslims.

The family is warm and generous towards their German visitor, almost to the point of embracing him. Only once does the conver-sation come to an abrupt halt, when the guest asks whether there was any truth in what he had read in old letters: that Helmy was not only of Muslim descent, but also had a German mother?

The question prompts a surly response from Helmy's great-nephew Ahmed Nur el-Din Farghal. That was just a rumour, the ex-officer snaps: mean-spirited denunciations by people trying to make out that Helmy was half-Jewish. He eyes the German visitor suspiciously, as if he has been too quick to trust him. Up to now, they have been chatting away easily in English, but now he probes a little further: what kind of accent is that, incidentally? American?

The truth is that the 'rumour' was fabricated by Helmy himself—in autumn 1939, when he needed to find a way out of his Gestapo basement prison. 'My mother is German', he had pleaded back then in letters to the Foreign Office and to Hitler. In the circumstances, he was bound to have clutched at any straw.[6] 'I, Mohd Helmy, a medical doctor specializing in internal diseases, was born on 25.7.1901 in Khartoum (Egypt) to a German mother', he writes at one point. And elsewhere: 'I am a German-Egyptian opposed to the English, and with an undying love of my motherland.'[7] He clearly hoped that the invention of a part-German heritage would make the Nazis look favourably upon him. He probably also relied on the fact that his lie would be hard to uncover. As a foreigner, he was not obliged to keep a family register. After the war, when Helmy was no longer in such straits, he never repeated his claim to have descended from a German mother. On the contrary, he wrote explicitly that his 'parents were Egyptian',[8] and that his mother was 'Egyptian and a Muslim'.[9] Her name was Amina Reda Hassan el-Komi; the family in Cairo even produce some old photographs of her in traditional garb.

All the same, Helmy's great-nephew won't let the matter rest, and insists on dispelling all doubts. It was, he says, precisely because Helmy was a Muslim and an Arab that he was quick to foresee the consequences of the 'Jewish war', as he calls the Second World War.

Everyone knew where it would all lead. Jews would come to Palestine, and problems would ensue. That was why Muslims had to act and stop Hitler in his tracks. Just as Helmy had done.

New York. The sun is dazzling, casting razor-sharp shadows between the glass façades of midtown Manhattan's high-rise buildings. Pedestrians teeter home, pulled along by small dogs.

The apartment is seventeen storeys up in the elevator; a wooden mezuzah scroll hangs at an angle from the doorpost. A large Jewish family—the Gutmans—is gathered here. It's a bit of a squash. People are sharing food, laughing. Photo albums are fetched, along with a black-and-white portrait of a serene, sturdy woman with dark hair.

'Our grandmother'. Clearly much-loved. Her name was Anna. The resemblance to her daughter is striking. Carla Gutman Greenspan, born 1956, explains how her mother survived the Nazis and the war in the heart of Hitler's capital city, and all thanks to a brave Egyptian Muslim. 'If Dr Helmy hadn't existed, this room, filled with twenty-five people, would simply be empty.'

Helmy must have been glad to know what a good life Anna was able to make for herself in the USA after the war. 'You can get everything in the stores, and there are more windowpanes in a single street than in the whole of Berlin', Anna wrote in a letter following her arrival in New York in 1946.

'Sailing into NY is unforgettable—so beautiful. An hour away from NY, you pass the Statue of Liberty on an island in the sea. It's an amazing sight. Everyone who has sailed past it so far has cried. You really feel like you're entering a free country.'[10]

After the war, Anna reported from her new home: 'I am working for a cousin of the Blumensteins. Her name is Silvia Berman. Her mother is the Blumensteins' mother's sister, in other words a maternal cousin…The cousin herself is a wonderful person. She has been to university and her husband is a doctor. A specialist in internal diseases. She has two very nice children, aged two and eleven. I am happy and very contented with my lot.' Anna was not the only one in her family to make a new start in the USA. Her mother and stepfather, Julie and Georg Wehr, also followed her

**Fig. 11.** A distant memory: the Rudniks' greengrocery on the Alexanderplatz before 'Aryanization'

over. But, as Anna wrote in a letter home, 'I'm the only one who has settled in so quickly.'[11]

Immediately after the end of the war, she had met the Polish Jew Chaim Gutman in Berlin, and the pair had fallen in love. Anna was twenty-two at the time. Writing in 1947 to her beloved Chaim, who had initially stayed behind in Berlin, she complains: 'I have heard nothing from my parents. As you know, they went to Detroit on Sunday and there's been no word from them yet.' In her letter, she appeals to him to come out and join her soon in the USA: 'You can only make a life here as a couple.' She describes her employer, the doctor and father of two, as generous, friendly, and decent. 'They tell me to make myself at home here, and I must say, I am treated very well. The family, she adds, 'reminds me very much of Dr Helmy'.[12]

The stars are soon twinkling over midtown Manhattan, but it is still light in the living room, where the family sits among embroidered cushions and gold picture frames. For a moment, it evokes memories of the living room in Cairo. And eventually another similarity emerges: just as the Cairo family don't know any Jews personally, so the New York family don't know any Muslims either. Anna's son, Charles Gutman, shares videos on Facebook, including one about Islam's alleged glorification of violence, entitled 'Son of Hamas Founder Says "Allah" of Koran is the Biggest Terrorist'.

Anna's daughter Carla talks about her and Charles's experiences of growing up in New York in the sixties. 'We lived in a neighbourhood where we had as many Italian Catholic friends as Jewish ones. We had an aunt who was mixed-race. We didn't distinguish between Catholics, Jews, Muslims, blacks, or whites. They were all just people to us.' It was a shame, she said, that the Arab countries didn't see it that way, and objected to having Jews live amongst them.

Anna's daughter has written a letter, and asks if it could be delivered to Helmy's descendants in Cairo. In it, she says: 'All I really want is for you to know that there is a family at the other end of the world that feels gratitude and love for Dr Helmy. We will never cease to be amazed by what he did, and we hope that his heroism will be an inspiration to others.'

# NOTES

## Chapter 1

1. Based on documents from the Gutman family archive, New York, and interviews with Carla Gutman Greenspan und Charles Gutman in September 2016.
2. Rumpelstilzchen ('Rumpelstiltskin', aka Adolf Stein), 'Ein Gespräch mit Professor Abdullah am Fehrbelliner Platz', Polemic No. 14, 13 December 1928, in Rumpelstilzchen, *Ja, hätt'ste…*, Berlin 1929.
3. Ibid. Alfred Kerr, letter of 3 May 1896, published in *Wo liegt Berlin? Briefe aus der Reichshauptstadt*, Berlin 1999, pp. 151–2, quoted in Aischa Ahmed, 'Die Sichtbarkeit ist eine Falle. Arabische Präsenzen, Völkerschauen und die Frage der gesellschaftlich Anderen in Deutschland (1896/1927)', in José Brunner and Shai Lavi (eds), *Juden und Muslime in Deutschland. Recht, Religion, Identität*. Tel Aviver Jahrbuch für deutsche Geschichte, 2009, pp. 81–102 (94 *passim*).
4. Rumpelstilzchen, 'Tripolitaner im Zoo', Polemic No. 40, 9 June 1927, in Rumpelstilzchen, *Berliner Funken*, Berlin 1927.
5. Paul Lindenberg and Hans Lichtenfelt, *Pracht-Album Photographischer Aufnahmen der Berliner Gewerbe-Ausstellung 1896 und der Sehenswürdigkeiten Berlins und des Treptower Parks, Alt-Berlin, Kolonial-Ausstellung, Kairo etc.* Berlin 1896, p. 48, quoted in Ahmed, 'Die Sichtbarkeit ist eine Falle'.
6. N.N., 'In der Berliner Gewerbe-Ausstellung', *Allgemeine Zeitung des Judenthums*, 5 June 1896.

## Chapter 3

1. Interview of September 2016 with Carla Gutman Greenspan.
2. Christian Pross/Rolf Winau (eds), *Nicht mißhandeln. Das Krankenhaus Moabit. 1920–1933. Ein Zentrum jüdischer Ärzte in Berlin. 1933–1945 Verfolgung, Widerstand, Zerstörung*, Berlin 1984, pp. 180–184.
3. Quoted in ibid., p. 180.
4. See ibid., p. 184.
5. Dr Karl Stern, quoted in ibid., p. 111 f.

6. According to a police clearance certificate dated 9 April 1937, Helmy was registered as resident in Berlin from 5 October 1922: archives of Humboldt University of Berlin, Medical Faculty I (1810–1945), 1049, fol. 41.

7. Yvan Goll, *Sodome et Berlin*, Paris 1929, translated extract by *Donald Nicholson-Smith* published in *The Brooklyn Rail*, April 2007.

8. Salim Abd al-Magid in the Cairo newspaper *al-Afkar*, 4 February 1920; quoted in Gerhard Höpp, 'Zwischen Universität und Straße. Ägyptische Studenten in Deutschland 1849–1945', in Konrad Schliephake/Ghazi Shanneik (eds), *Die Beziehungen zwischen der Bundesrepublik Deutschland und der Arabischen Republik Ägypten*, Würzburg 2002, pp. 31–41, here p. 32.

9. Interview of May 2016 with Prof. Nasser Kotby and photographs from Helmy's estate showing white wine and beer glasses.

10. See Gerdien Jonker, 'The forgotten experiment. German-Muslim elective affinities in the interwar period', in Claudia Schmidt-Hahn (ed.), *Islam verstehen – Herausforderung für Europa*, Innsbruck 2015, pp. 35–41, here p. 36.

11. See ibid., p. 36 f.

12. See Susannah Heschel, 'German Jewish Scholarship on Islam as a Tool for De-Orientalizing Judaism', *New German Critique* 117 (2012), pp. 91–107.

13. Letter of 13 April 1937 from NSDAP headquarters, *Amt Rosenberg*, to the head of the Berlin police department; see Marc David Baer, 'Muslim Encounters with Nazism and the Holocaust: The Ahmadi of Berlin and Jewish Convert to Islam Hugo Marcus', in *The American Historical Review* (2015) 120 (I) pp. 140–171, here p. 160.

14. Ibid.

15. See ibid., p. 150.

16. See Chalid-Albert Seiler-Chan, 'Der Islam in Berlin und anderwärts im deutschen Reiche', *Moslemische Revue*, October 1934, pp. 112–119, here p. 115. Portrait photograph in the same issue.

17. See ibid., p. 114. On Seiler-Chan's biography, see Gerdien Jonker, *The Ahmadiyya Quest for Religious Progress*, Leiden 2016, p. 146.

18. Rumpelstilzchen ('Rumpelstiltskin', aka Adolf Stein), 'Die Moschee aus der Vogelschau – Dr Abdullah vom Fehrbelliner Platz', Polemic No. 38 of 31 May 1934, Rumpelstilzchen, *Sie wer'n lachen!*, Berlin 1934.

19. Marc David Baer, 'Muslim Encounters with Nazism and the Holocaust: The Ahmadi of Berlin and Jewish Convert to Islam Hugo Marcus', in *The American Historical Review* (2015) 120 (I), pp. 140–171, here p. 157.

20. See report from the newspaper *Der Tag*, reproduced in excerpts in *Moslemische Revue*, October 1934, p. 92.
21. See *Vossische Zeitung*, 19 February 1931; *Deutsche Allgemeine Zeitung/Berliner Rundschau*, 19 February 1931.
22. Report from the newspaper *Der Tag*, reproduced in excerpts in *Moslemische Revue*, October 1934, p. 92.
23. Helmy also received his medical licence on 26 November 1931; this was preceded by a practical year, however, so the date was predictable well in advance. See medical career file Dr Helmy, Berlin State Archive, B Rep. 012, No. 1376.
24. Walther Rathenau, *Die schönste Stadt der Welt*, new edition, Hamburg 2015, p. 20.
25. See interview of May 2016 with Prof. Nasser Kotby.
26. Reference of 28 March 1933 for Dr M. Helmy by Prof. Georg Klemperer, medical career file Dr Helmy, Berlin State Archive, B Rep. 012, No. 1376.
27. See interview of 31 January 1984 with Peter Fleischmann in Haifa, quoted in Pross/Winau, *Nicht mißhandeln*, p. 119.
28. Ibid.
29. Reference of 1 August 1937 for Dr M. Helmy by Prof. Werner Sieber, medical career file Dr Helmy, Berlin State Archive, B Rep. 012, No. 1376. fol. 11.
30. Reference of 28 March 1933 for Dr M. Helmy by Prof. Georg Klemperer, medical career file Dr Helmy, Berlin State Archive, B Rep. 012, No. 1376.
31. See estate of Prof. Dr Gerhard Höpp, Centre for Modern Oriental Studies, Berlin, 07.02.066.
32. See Christian Pross/Rolf Winau (eds), *Nicht mißhandeln*, p. 117 f.
33. Pross/Winau, *Nicht mißhandeln*, p. 180.
34. Compensation case file Helmy, Berlin State Administration Office, Compensation Board (LABO Berlin), Reg. No. 14 500, fol. C 10, M 11.
35. See Robert-Koch-Institut (ed.), *Verfolgte Ärzte im Nationalsozialismus. Dokumentation zur Ausstellung über das SA-Gefängnis General-Pape-Straße*, Berlin 1999, p. 53.
36. See Pross/Winau, *Nicht mißhandeln*, p. 143.
37. Ibid., p. 181.
38. See ibid.
39. See ibid., p. 187; Dr Helmy's affidavit of 9 February 1953 for submission to the Compensation Board; notarized copy in LABO Berlin, Reg. No. 14 500, fol. C 10–16.

40. See Gerdien Jonker, 'The forgotten experiment. German-Muslim elective affinities in the interwar period', Claudia Schmidt-Hahn, *Islam verstehen – Herausforderung für Europa*, Innsbruck 2015, pp. 35–41, here p. 36 f.

41. See Gerdien Jonker, *The Ahmadiyya Quest for Religious Progress*, Leiden 2016, pp. 142–144.

42. See Marc David Baer, 'Muslim Encounters with Nazism and the Holocaust: The Ahmadi of Berlin and Jewish Convert to Islam Hugo Marcus', in *The American Historical Review* (2015) 120 (I), pp. 140–171, here p. 155.

43. See ibid., p. 147.

44. See ibid., p. 156.

45. See Manfred Backhausen (ed.), *Die Lahore-Ahmadiyya-Bewegung in Europa*, Wembley 2008, p. 114.

46. See Baer, 'Muslim Encounters', p. 156.

47. Rumpelstilzchen, 'Deutsche Mohammedanerinnen', Polemic No. 14 of 13 December 1928, Rumpelstilzchen, *Ja hätt'ste...*, Berlin 1929.

48. Hugo Marcus, 'Spinoza und der Islam', *Moslemische Revue*, January 1929, pp. 8–24, here p. 9.

49. See Robert-Koch-Institut (ed.), *Verfolgte Ärzte im Nationalsozialismus*, p. 53.

50. In his compensation claim after the war, Helmy himself presented this as a postdoctoral position, making his career—which came to an abrupt end in 1937—appear even more brilliant. In actual fact, he did not gain his doctorate until 1937: archives of Humboldt University of Berlin, Med. Fac. I (1810–1945), 1049, fols. 37–41, here fol. 42.

51. See Pross/Winau, *Nicht mißhandeln*, p. 198.

52. Photograph in el-Kelish family archive.

53. Dr Karl Stern, quoted in Pross/Winau, *Nicht mißhandeln*, p. 112.

## Chapter 4

1. Dr Karl Stern, quoted in Pross/Winau, *Nicht mißhandeln*, pp. 203 and 206.

2. Dr Helmy's affidavit of 9 February 1953 for submission to the Compensation Board; notarized copy in LABO Berlin, Reg. No. 14 500, fols. C 10–16.

3. Letter of 10 November 1936 from F. Reuter, Chief Pharmacist, Central Health Office, Foreign Office Political Archive, R 27 262.

4. Adolf Hitler, *Mein Kampf*, Munich 1930, p. 602; quoted in Klaus-Michael Mallmann/Martin Cüppers, *Nazi Palestine: The Plans for the Extermination of the Jews in Palestine*, trans. Krista Smith, New York 2010, p. 32.

5. Gerhard Höpp, 'Zwischen Universität und Straße. Ägyptische Studenten in Deutschland 1849–1945', in Konrad Schliephake/Ghazi Shanneik (eds), *Die Beziehungen zwischen der Bundesrepublik Deutschland und der Arabischen Republik Ägypten*, Würzburg 2002, pp. 31–41, here p. 39 f.

6. Ibid.

7. See David Motadel, *Islam and Nazi Germany's War*, Cambridge, Massachusetts/London 2014, p. 57.

8. See ibid.

9. See letter of 10 November 1936 from F. Reuter, Chief Pharmacist, Central Health Office, Foreign Office Political Archive, R27262, and reference of 1 August 1937 for Dr M. Helmy by Prof. Sieber, medical career file Dr Helmy, Berlin State Archive, B Rep. 012, No. 1376, fol.11.

10. Medical career file Dr Helmy, Berlin State Archive, B Rep. 012, No. 1376, fol.10.

11. See David Motadel, *Islam and Nazi Germany's War*, Cambridge, Massachusetts/London 2014, p. 58.

12. Interview of May 2016 with Mervat el-Kashab.

13. Interview of May 2016 with Mohamed el-Kashab and Mervat el-Kashab.

14. Reference of 30 September 1934 for Dr M. Helmy by Prof. Schilling, Foreign Office Political Archive, R 8045.

## Chapter 5

1. See Pross/Winau, *Nicht mißhandeln*, p. 206.

2. Ibid., p. 221.

3. 'Die SA als Garant der Zukunft', *Der SA-Mann*, Year 3, 17 February 1934, p. 1 f., quoted in Pross/Winau, *Nicht mißhandeln*, p. 194 f.

4. Pross/Winau, *Nicht mißhandeln*, p. 206 f.

5. See ibid., p. 207.

6. Ibid.

7. Letter of 13 December 1937 from Prof. Helmut Dennig to the Berlin Physicians' Chamber, Foreign Office Political Archive, R27262. For more on Dennig, see also Klaus Dörner/Angelika Ebbinghaus/Karsten Linne (eds), *Der Nürnberger Ärzteprozeß 1946/47*, Munich 2000, p. 88.

8. See Peter Schütt, 'Preußens Gloria und die Grüne Fahne des Propheten', in *Mut. Forum für Kultur, Politik und Geschichte* 362 (1997), pp. 40–51, here p. 50.

9. Carl Seelig (ed.), *Helle Zeit—dunkle Zeit. In memoriam Albert Einstein*, Zurich 1956, p. 55.

10. Zaki Aly, 'Die arabische Kultur im 10. Jahrhundert', *Moslemische Revue*, January 1934, p. 18.

11. See Gerhard Höpp, 'Die Sache ist von immenser Wichtigkeit...'. Arabische Studenten in Berlin. Manuscript from the estate of Prof. Dr Gerhard Höpp, Centre for Modern Oriental Studies, Berlin, 07.08.005, p. 20.

12. See Marc David Baer, 'Muslim Encounters with Nazism and the Holocaust: The Ahmadi of Berlin and Jewish Convert to Islam Hugo Marcus', in *The American Historical Review* (2015) 120 (I), pp. 140–171, here p. 148.

13. Carl Krug, 'Die Sonder-Ausstellung Kairo', in Fritz Kühnemann, B. Fehlisch, L. M. Goldberger (eds), 'Berlin und seine Arbeit. Amtlicher Bericht der Berliner Gewerbe-Ausstellung 1896', Berlin 1896, pp. 867–873, here p. 871; quoted in Aischa Ahmed, '"Die Sichtbarkeit ist eine Falle'. Arabische Präsenzen, Völkerschauen und die Frage des gesellschaftlich Anderen in Deutschland (1896/1927)", in José Brunner/ Shai Lavi (eds), 'Juden und Muslime in Deutschland. Recht, Religion, Identität', *Tel Aviver Jahrbuch für deutsche Geschichte*, Göttingen 2009, pp. 81–102, here p. 96.

14. Letter of 13 December 1937 from Prof. Helmut Dennig to the Berlin Physicians' Chamber, Foreign Office Political Archive, R27262.

15. According to an account given to the Berlin physician Dr Karsten Mülder by a former receptionist who worked for Helmy after the war.

16. Interview of May 2016 with Prof. Nasser Kotby.

17. Walther Rathenau, *Die schönste Stadt der Welt*, new edition, Hamburg 2015, p. 26.

18. Rumpelstilzchen ('Rumpelstiltskin', aka Adolf Stein), 'Dr Abdullah vom Fehrbelliner Platz', Polemic No. 38 of 31 May 1934, in Rumpelstilzchen, *Sie wer'n lachen!*, Berlin 1934.

19. See Christian Pross/Rolf Winau (eds), *Nicht mißhandeln*, p. 207.

20. Ibid., p. 215 f.

21. Ibid., p. 210.

22. Letter of 12 December 1937 from Prof. Werner Sieber to the hospital management, Foreign Office Political Archive, R27262.

23. Letter of 13 December 1937 from Prof. Helmut Dennig to the Berlin Physicians' Chamber, Foreign Office Political Archive, R27262.
24. Dr Helmy's affidavit of 9 February 1953 for submission to the Compensation Board, notarized copy in Berlin State Administration Office, Compensation Board (LABO Berlin), Reg. No. 14 500, fols. C 10–16.
25. Julie Wehr's report of 26 September 1945, Yad Vashem Archives, M. 31/12582.
26. Letter of 25 October 1948 from Cecilie Rudnik to Anna, Gutman family archive.
27. Memorandum of 7 December 1939 by Werner Otto von Hentig, Foreign Office Envoy to the Middle East, Foreign Office Political Archive, R27262.
28. Letter of 13 December 1937 from Prof. Helmut Dennig to the Berlin Physicians' Chamber, Foreign Office Political Archive, R27262.
29. Letter of 12 December 1937 from Prof. Werner Sieber to the hospital management, Foreign Office Political Archive, R27262.
30. Dr Helmy's affidavit of 9 February 1953 for submission to the Compensation Board, notarized copy in Berlin State Administration Office, Compensation Board (LABO Berlin), Reg. No. 14 500, fols. C 10–16.
31. Ibid.
32. Ibid.

## Chapter 6

1. The fact that the life stories of these (in some cases only temporary) tenants have been rescued from oblivion is thanks to the couple Sabine Mülder and Dr Karsten Mülder, whose unpublished research has resulted in the laying of *Stolpersteine* (cobblestone-sized individual memorials) in front of Krefelder Straße 7. The results were presented at the unveiling of a memorial plaque to Helmy on 4 July 2014, at which the author was present.
2. Dr Helmy's affidavit of 9 February 1953 for submission to the Compensation Board, notarized copy in Berlin State Administration Office, Compensation Board (LABO Berlin), Reg. No. 14 500, fols. C 10–16.
3. Compensation case file Anna Boros, LABO Berlin, Reg. No. 52 472, fol. E 5.
4. Anna's autobiographical account of 1 November 1945, Yad Vashem Archives, M. 31/12582.

5. Anna writes after the war that the Jewish school at Auguststraße 11–13 where she was enrolled was finally closed down in 1939 or 1940. In actual fact, it continued to operate until 30 January 1942: see Jörg H. Fehrs, *Von der Heidereutergasse zum Roseneck. Jüdische Schulen in Berlin 1712–1942*, Berlin 1993, p. 118. On this particular school, see also Regina Scheer, *Ahawah. Das vergessene Haus*, Berlin 1993, p. 9, and appendix.

6. See Paragraph 2, Article 2 of the Eighth Supplementary Decree to the Reich Citizenship Law of 17 January 1939 (RGBl. I, p. 47): Jews working in any of the auxiliary medical professions (as defined in Paragraph 1, Article 1 of the law of 28 September 1938 on nursing, RGBl. I p. 1309) were only allowed to practise their profession 'on Jews or in Jewish institutions'.

7. Anna's autobiographical account of 1 November 1945, Yad Vashem Archives, M. 31/12582. Helmy himself does not mention any of these three names in the memoirs and personal accounts he wrote after the war. The first can be assumed to refer to Aron Arthur and Gertrud Conitzer, who—like Helmy—lived at Krefelder Straße 7. Both were deported to Auschwitz on 12 January 1943 and murdered there. See Zentralinstitut für sozialwissenschaftliche Forschung der Freien Universität Berlin (ed.), *Gedenkbuch Berlins der jüdischen Opfer des Nationalsozialismus*, Berlin 1995. The names Benatzky and Oppenheimer could not be traced.

8. Anna's autobiographical account of 1 November 1945, Yad Vashem Archives, M. 31/12582.

9. Dr Helmy's affidavit of 9 February 1953 for submission to the Compensation Board, notarized copy in State Administration Office, Compensation Board (LABO Berlin), Reg. No. 14 500, fols. C 10–16.

10. See ibid.

11. See reference of 30 September 1934 for Dr Helmy by Prof. Schilling, Foreign Office Political Archive, R 8045.

12. Kurt Pätzold/Manfred Weißbecker, *Rudolf Heß. Der Mann an Hitlers Seite*, Leipzig 1999, p. 17.

13. Compensation case file Helmy, LABO Berlin, Reg. No. 14 500, fol. C 5. The claim that Helmy had attended the same school as Hess was indeed only a rumour. There was an age difference of several years between Helmy and the Hess brothers, and they had lived in different cities: Hess in Alexandria, and Helmy—according to the interviews of May 2016 with Nasser Kotby and Ahmed Farghal—in Giza, Tanta, and

Cairo. Moreover, Rudolf Hess had only attended his Protestant primary school in Egypt for a year before continuing his schooling with private tutors: see Pätzold/Weißbecker, *Rudolf Heß*, p. 17. Helmy's insistence that the rumour had not been spread by him, but by someone who wanted to damage his reputation, is also credible. Indeed, he continued to assert this even after the war, when it would have been to his advantage to present himself as a derider of the Nazis.

14. See previous chapter.

15. Letter of 9 November 1939 from the head of the NSDAP Foreign Organization (AO) to the Berlin police headquarters, and Foreign Office memorandum of 16 November 1939, Foreign Office Political Archive, R27262.

16. Ibid.

17. Foreign Office memorandum of 16 May 1941, Foreign Office Political Archive, R 29863.

18. Foreign Office memorandum of 17 November 1939, Foreign Office Political Archive, R27262.

19. See Werner Otto von Hentig, *Mein Leben. Eine Dienstreise*, Göttingen 1962, p. 332.

20. See ibid., p. 332 ff.

21. Ibid. Foreign Office letter of 30 September 1939 ('Very Urgent'), Foreign Office Political Archive, R27262. Memorandum of 10 October 1939 from the *Wehrmacht* High Command, Foreign Office Political Archive, R27262: 'As a retaliatory measure for the internment of citizens of the German Reich in Egypt, a number of Egyptians have been interned in Germany. It is requested that an investigation be conducted into whether it would not be expedient to release the Egyptian detainees and intern British nationals instead. The case for such a measure is that the detention of the Germans in Egypt took place as a result of British pressure; furthermore, the release of the Egyptians would have favourable political consequences for Germany in Egypt.'

22. Foreign Office letter of 30 September 1939 ('Very Urgent'), Foreign Office Political Archive, R27262.

## Chapter 7

1. See Jani Pietsch, *'Ich besaß einen Garten in Schöneiche bei Berlin'. Das verwaltete Verschwinden jüdischer Nachbarn und ihre schwierige Rückkehr*, Frankfurt/New York 2006, p. 101.

2. See Julie Wehr's report of 26 September 1945, Yad Vashem Archives, M.31, 12582. Date according to Pietsch, *Garten in Schöneiche*, p. 101.
3. Anna's report of 10 July 1945, Yad Vashem Archives, M. 31/12582.
4. See Julie Wehr's report of 26 September 1945, Yad Vashem Archives, M.31, 12582. Date according to Pietsch, *Garten in Schöneiche*, p. 104.
5. See ibid. Letter of 6 November 1947 from Julie Wehr to Henry Gutman, Gutman family archive.
6. See letter of 6 November 1947 from Julie Wehr to Henry Gutman, Gutman family archive.
7. See compensation case file Cecilie Rudnik, LABO Berlin, Reg. No. 25535, fol. C 8.
8. Foreign Office memorandum of 23 February 1940, Foreign Office Political Archive, R 13637.
9. In some eyewitness accounts, this is misspelt Wühlsburg; for the correct spelling, see the Foreign Office Political Archive, R 27262 (e.g. camp doctor's stamp or correspondence between the Gestapo and Foreign Office).
10. The selection of those to be detained was left to the Gestapo, according to a memorandum of 5 October 1939 issued by the Foreign Office envoy to the Middle East, Werner Otto von Hentig, Foreign Office Political Archive, R27262.
11. Foreign Office record ('Confidential') of 4 December 1939, Foreign Office Political Archive, R27262.
12. See letter of 5 October 1939 from Werner Otto von Hentig to Under-Secretary of State Woermann, and letter of 28 October 1939 from the Berlin Islamic Community to Hentig, both in the FO Political Archive, R 41394.
13. Letter of 9 November 1939 from the head of the NSDAP Foreign Organization (AO) to the Berlin police headquarters, and letter of 17 November 1939 from the Foreign Office to the Gestapo, Foreign Office Political Archive, R 27262.
14. Dr Helmy was in fact the first to be released, having succeeded in engineering an exchange with the aid of some Muslim diplomats. Under this arrangement, two German detainees in Egypt who, like himself, had fallen ill, were released for medical treatment, and the same concession was granted to Helmy in return. Memorandum of 24 May 1940 issued by Theodor Habicht, Under-Secretary of State at the Foreign Office, Foreign Office Political Archive, R 7620.
15. See memorandum of 29 April 1941, Foreign Office Political Archive, R 29863.

16. See letter of 30 May 1941 from Kamal el-Din Galal to Werner Otto von Hentig, Foreign Office Political Archive, R 29863.

17. Memorandum of 25 October 1940 by Alfred Hess, Foreign Office Political Archive, R 29863.

18. Interview of May 2016 with Ahmed Farghal.

19. Anna's report of 10 July 1945, Yad Vashem Archives, M. 31, 12582.

20. Ibid.

21. See Anna's letters, Gutman family archive.

22. See photograph in Wehr's victim-of-fascism identification card, compensation case file Georg Wehr, LABO Berlin, Reg. No. 71 761.

23. Letter of 8 April 1950 from Martin Rudnik to Anna Gutman, Gutman family archive.

24. See compensation case file Georg Wehr, LABO Berlin, Reg. No. 71 761, fol. C 2.

25. See Beate Kosmala, 'Mißglückte Hilfe und ihre Folgen: Die Ahndung der "Judenbegünstigung" durch NS-Verfolgungsbehörden', in Beate Kosmala/Claudia Schoppmann (eds), *Überleben im Untergrund. Hilfe für Juden in Deutschland 1941–1945*, Berlin 2002, pp. 205–221, here p. 209 f.

26. See compensation case file Georg Wehr, LABO Berlin, Reg. No. 71 761, fol. M 13.

27. Letter of 21 March 1938 from Dr Müller, ibid., fol. E 5.

28. Compensation case file Cecilie Rudnik, LABO Berlin, Reg. No. 25 535, fol. M 6. On the liquidation of the business, see database 'Jewish Businesses in Berlin 1930–1945' in the Berlin State Archive, entry M. Rudnik GmbH. For interpretation, see also Jani Pietsch, *'Ich besaß einen Garten in Schöneiche bei Berlin'*, p. 103.

29. Compensation case file Georg Wehr, LABO Berlin, Reg. No. 71 761, fol. M 14.

30. Ibid., fol. M 14, B 29, E 11.

31. See ibid., fol. M 14.

32. See Anna's report of 10 July 1945, Yad Vashem Archives M. 31, 12582.

33. Ibid. This is contradicted by Julie's story that the whole thing was settled between Helmy and Georg Wehr by telephone; see Julie Wehr's report of 26 September 1945, Yad Vashem Archives, M. 31/12582. Julie's version seems less likely, however, given the heightened precautions Anna refers to regarding phone calls.

34. Anna's report of 10 July 1945, Yad Vashem Archives, M. 31/12582.

35. See compensation case file Martin Rudnik, LABO Berlin, Reg. No. 23973, fol. C 8f., C 10, D 28.

36. See ibid., fol. M 17. This distinction persisted in German dentistry until 1952. Unlike a *Zahnarzt*, a *Dentist* had no academic training.
37. See ibid., fol. E 3.
38. See ibid., fol. M 17.
39. See ibid., fols. D 27–28.
40. See ibid., fol. D 18.
41. See ibid., fols. D 27–28.
42. Julie Wehr's report of 26 September 1945, Yad Vashem Archives, M. 31/12582.
43. Anna's handwritten autobiographical account, December 1953, Berlin State Archive, B Rep. 078, No. 0561 ('Unsung Heroes' collection, application Mohd Helmy), fols. 13–16, here fol. 14.
44. Anna's compensation case file, LABO Berlin, Reg. No. 52472, fol. C 45.

## Chapter 8

1. See Anna's compensation case file, LABO Berlin, Reg. No. 52472, fol. C 40.
2. Anna's report of 10 July 1945, Yad Vashem Archives, M. 31/12582.
3. Anna's handwritten autobiographical account of December 1953, Berlin State Archive, B Rep. 078, No. 0561 ('Unsung Heroes' collection, application Mohd Helmy), fols. 13–16.
4. Anna's handwritten autobiographical account, 1 November 1945, Yad Vashem Archives, M. 31/12582.
5. See Radu Ioanid, *The Holocaust in Romania. The Destruction of Jews and Gypsies Under the Antonescu Regime, 1940–1944*, Chicago 2000, pp. 259–270.
6. Anna's handwritten autobiographical account, December 1953, Berlin State Archive, B Rep. 078, No. 0561 ('Unsung Heroes' collection, application Mohd Helmy), fols. 13–16.
7. Anna's report of 10 July 1945, Yad Vashem Archives, M. 31/12582.
8. Anna's handwritten autobiographical account, December 1953, Berlin State Archive, B Rep. 078, No. 0561 ('Unsung Heroes' collection, application Mohd Helmy), fols. 13–16.
9. Anna's report of 10 July 1945, Yad Vashem Archives, M. 31/12582.
10. Ibid.
11. Cecilie Rudnik's handwritten autobiographical account of 5 November 1945, Berlin State Archive, C Rep. 118–01, No. 35 340.
12. See letter from Helene Mattisson to Anna Gutman, 10 September 1948, Gutman family archive.

13. See Jani Pietsch, *'Ich besaß einen Garten in Schöneiche bei Berlin'. Das verwaltete Verschwinden jüdischer Nachbarn und ihre schwierige Rückkehr*, Frankfurt/New York 2006, p. 104.

14. Julie Wehr's report of 26 September 1945, Yad Vashem Archives, M. 31/12582.

15. Anna's autobiographical account of 1 November 1945, Yad Vashem Archives, M. 31/12582.

16. Anna's handwritten autobiographical account of December 1953, Berlin State Archive, B Rep. 078, No. 0561 ('Unsung Heroes' collection, application Mohd Helmy), fols. 13–16, here 14 f.

17. Ibid., fol. 14.

18. Interviews of September 2016 with Carla Gutman Greenspan and Charles Gutman.

## Chapter 9

1. Interviews of September 2016 with Carla Gutman Greenspan and Charles Gutman.

2. Ibid.

3. Foreign Office memorandum of 29 April 1941, Foreign Office Political Archive, R 29863.

4. Anna's handwritten autobiographical account of December 1953, Berlin State Archive, B Rep. 078, No. 0561 ('Unsung Heroes' collection, application Mohd Helmy), fols. 13–16, here 15, and interviews of September 2016 with Carla Gutman Greenspan and Charles Gutman.

5. Interviews of September 2016 with Carla Gutman Greenspan and Charles Gutman.

6. Pamphlet 'Muselmannen', *c.*1944, German Federal Archives, Military Archive, RS 3–39/1, quoted in David Motadel, *Islam and Nazi Germany's War*, Cambridge, Massachusetts/London 2014, p. 250.

7. Helmy's letter of 8 December 1939 to Hitler, Foreign Office Political Archive, R 27262.

8. Memorandum of 19 November 1939 by Martin Bormann, Foreign Office Political Archive, R 27262.

9. Letter of 17 November 1939 from the Foreign Office to the Gestapo, Foreign Office Political Archive, R 27262.

10. Helmy was released from detention from 8 December 1939 to 5 January 1940. Memorandum of 24 October 1940 by Alfred Hess and memorandum of 26 April 1941, Foreign Office Political Archive, R 29863.

11. Letter of 13.13.1939 [sic] from Helmy to Consul Dr Melches, Foreign Office Political Archive, R 27262.

12. Circular No. 124/43 of 2 September 1943, Führer's headquarters, Federal Archives Berlin, NS 6/342.

13. See political clearance certificate for submission to Foreign Office, NSDAP *Gau Berlin, Kreis IV, Ortsgruppe Wiking*, 13 December 1939, Foreign Office Political Archive, R 27262.

14. Letter of 12 November 1936 from the Ministry of Propaganda to the Foreign Office, Foreign Office Political Archive, R 121232.

15. See Marc David Baer, 'Muslim Encounters with Nazism and the Holocaust: The Ahmadi of Berlin and Jewish Convert to Islam Hugo Marcus', in *The American Historical Review* (2015) 120 (I), pp. 140–171, here p. 159.

16. See ibid.

17. See ibid., pp. 158–160.

18. See Manfred Backhausen, *Die Lahore-Ahmadiyya-Bewegung in Europa*, Wembley 2008, p. 77.

19. Interviews of September 2016 with Carla Gutman Greenspan and Charles Gutman.

20. See letter of 12 August 1947 from Anna Gutman to Henry Gutman, Gutman family archive.

21. Interviews of September 2016 with Carla Gutman Greenspan and Charles Gutman.

22. Letter of 16 April 1940 from Emmy Ernst to Joachim von Ribbentrop, Foreign Office Political Archive, R 8045.

23. Letter of 16 April 1940 from Emmy Ernst to Hitler, Foreign Office Political Archive, R 8045.

24. See Beate Kosmala, 'Mißglückte Hilfe und ihre Folgen: Die Ahndung der "Judenbegünstigung" durch NS-Verfolgungsbehörden', in Beate Kosmala/Claudia Schoppmann (eds), *Überleben im Untergrund. Hilfe für Juden in Deutschland 1941–1945*, Berlin 2002, pp. 205–221, here p. 209, and Christian Dirks, '"Greifer". Der Fahndungsdienst der Berliner Gestapo', in Beate Meyer/Hermann Simon (eds), *Juden in Berlin 1938–1945*, Berlin 2000, pp. 233–257.

25. Anna's handwritten autobiographical account of December 1953, Berlin State Archive, B Rep. 078, No. 0561 ('Unsung Heroes' collection, application Mohd Helmy), fols. 13–16, here fol. 15.

## Chapter 10

1. Interviews of September 2016 with Carla Gutman Greenspan and Charles Gutman.
2. Quoted in Klaus-Michael Mallmann/Martin Cüppers, *Nazi Palestine*, p. 96.
3. Quoted in ibid., p. 37.
4. See ibid.
5. David Motadel, *Islam and Nazi Germany's War*, Cambridge, Massachusetts/London 2014, p. 260.
6. M. N., 'Bajram u Našoj Diviziji: Zakleta Zajednica: Govor Zapoviednika i Divizijskog Imama Prilikom Bajramske Svečanosti', in *Handžar* 7, 1943, quoted in ibid., p. 255. The Handschar Division derived its name from the oriental scimitar.
7. See ibid., p. 42; Mallmann/Cüppers, *Nazi Palestine: The Plans for the Extermination of the Jews in Palestine*, trans. Krista Smith, New York, 2010, p. 91 f.
8. Motadel, *Islam and Nazi Germany's War*, p. 254 f.
9. Quoted in the memoirs of Himmler's masseur Felix Kersten, *Totenkopf und Treue. Heinrich Himmler ohne Uniform. Aus den Tagebuchblättern des finnischen Medizinalrats Felix Kersten*, Hamburg 1952, p. 203 (1 December 1942).
10. Mallmann/Cüppers, *Nazi Palestine*, p. 98.
11. Quoted in Gerhard Höpp (ed.), *Mufti-Papiere. Briefe, Memoranden, Reden und Aufrufe Amin al-Hussainis aus dem Exil, 1940–1945*, Berlin 2001, p. 233.
12. Quoted in Mallmann/Cüppers, *Nazi Palestine*, p. 90.
13. Interview of September 2016 with Charles Gutman.

## Chapter 11

1. N. N., 'Die Galal-Vorstellung', *Der Spiegel* No. 17/1959, 22 April 1959.
2. Mallmann/Cüppers, *Nazi Palestine*, p. 93.
3. See Gerhard Höpp, 'Zwischen Universität und Straße. Ägyptische Studenten in Deutschland 1849–1945', in Konrad Schliephake/Ghazi Shanneik (eds), *Die Beziehungen zwischen der Bundesrepublik Deutschland und der Arabischen Republik Ägypten*, Würzburg 2002, pp. 31–41, here p. 39.
4. See ibid., p. 41.

5. Letter with illegible signature, Foreign Office Political Archive, R 29863; see also estate of Prof. Dr Gerhard Höpp, Centre for Modern Oriental Studies, Berlin, 01.15.061.

6. Gerhard Höpp, *Zwischen Universität und Straße*, p. 40.

7. Long after the war, Helmy wrote 'I am Egyptian and a Muslim' in a letter to the Egyptian Consulate in Hamburg, dated 22 September 1962, Berlin, Dr Helmy's estate, el-Kelish family archive.

8. See Anna's compensation case file, LABO Berlin, Reg. No. 52 472, fol. C 12.

9. Interview of September 2016 with Carla Gutman Greenspan.

10. Letter of 23 February 1952 from Cecilie Rudnik and Martin Rudnik to Anna Gutman, Gutman family archive.

11. Letter of 8 April 1950 from Martin Rudnik to Anna Gutman, Gutman family archive.

12. See Foreign Office record of 4 December 1939 ('Confidential'), Foreign Office Political Archive, R 27262, and Gerhard Höpp, "Muslime unterm Hakenkreuz. Zur Entstehungsgeschichte des Islamischen Zentralinstituts zu Berlin e.V.", in *Moslemische Revue* 1 (1994), pp. 16–27.

13. See Gerhard Höpp, 'Der Koran als "Geheime Reichssache". Bruchstücke deutscher Islam-Politik zwischen 1938 und 1945', in Holger Preißler/ Hubert Seiwert (eds), *Gnosisforschung und Religionsgeschichte. Festschrift für Kurt Rudolph zum 65. Geburtstag*, Marburg 1994, pp. 435–446.

14. Sadr-ud-Din, 'Die Christen und die Juden', in *Moslemische Revue*, April 1924, p. 41 f.

15. Address of 21 April 1943, quoted in Klaus-Michael Mallmann/Martin Cüppers, *Nazi Palestine*, p. 96.

16. Quoted in ibid.

17. Quoted in ibid.

18. See letter of 26 February 1944 from Kamal el-Din Galal to Dr Schmidt-Dumont, Ministry of Propaganda, Foreign Department, from the estate of Prof. Dr Gerhard Höpp, Centre for Modern Oriental Studies, Berlin, 013/006.

19. Correspondence between the Ministry of Propaganda, Galal, and the Reich Main Security Office, fol. 54, from the estate of Prof. Dr Gerhard Höpp, Centre for Modern Oriental Studies, Berlin, 013/006.

20. Quoted in Albert Speer, trans. Richard and Clara Winston, *Inside the Third Reich*, London 1971, p. 96.

21. Quoted in Saul Friedländer, *Nazi Germany and the Jews: The Years of Persecution: 1933-1939*, London 1997, p. 102.

22. Ian Kershaw, *Hitler 1889–1936*, Munich 1998, at the end of Chapter VI.
23. Victor Klemperer, entry of 12 November 1944, in *Ich will Zeugnis ablegen bis zum letzten: Tagebücher 1941-1945, ed.* Walter Nowojski, Berlin 1995, p. 610.
24. See David Motadel, *Islam and Nazi Germany's War*, Cambridge, Massachusetts/London 2014, p. 278.
25. Yvan Goll, *Sodome et Berlin*, Paris 1929, translated extract by Donald Nicholson-Smith published in *The Brooklyn Rail*, April 2007.
26. Yvan Goll, *Sodome et Berlin*, Paris 1929. Quotation translated by Sharon Howe.
27. Sadr-ud-Din, 'Das Glaubensbekenntnis des Islam', in *Moslemische Revue* 1, April 1924, pp. 22–24, here p. 24.
28. Certificate of conversion, Berlin, 10 June 1943, Yad Vashem Archives, M. 31/12582.

## Chapter 12

1. See Irene Messinger, 'Schutz- und Scheinehen im Exilland Ägypten', in Margit Franz/Heimo Halbrainer/Gabriele Anderl (eds), *Going East. Going South. Österreichisches Exil in Asien und Afrika*, Graz 2013, pp. 165–182, here p. 167.
2. Public prosecutor's investigation file 1941, Berlin State Archive, A Rep. 358–02, No. 154335. Further details include date of birth, career, and income.
3. See Goll, *Sodome et Berlin*, translated extract by Donald Nicholson-Smith published in *The Brooklyn Rail*, April 2007.
4. See letter from Romanian Consulate General to Anna, Berlin, 4 November 1942, Yad Vashem Archives, M. 31/12582: 'With reference to your letter of 4th of this month, the Consulate General advises that it has no objection to your marriage to an Egyptian national.'
5. Letter of 28 June 1943 from the Swiss legation to Abdel Aziz Helmy Hammad, Berlin, Yad Vashem Archives, M. 31/12582.
6. See Julie Wehr's report of 26 September 1945, Yad Vashem Archives, M. 31/12582.
7. Anna's biographical account of Helmy, Berlin State Archive, B Rep. 078, No. 0561 ('Unsung Heroes' collection, application Mohd Helmy), fol. 17.
8. See Robert Satloff, *Among the Righteous. Lost Stories from the Holocaust's Long Reach into Arab Lands*, New York 2006, p. 171 f.

9. Thea Levinsohn-Wolf, *Stationen einer jüdischen Krankenschwester. Deutschland—Ägypten—Israel*, Frankfurt 1996, p. 48, and Irene Messinger, 'Schutz- und Scheinehen im Exilland Ägypten', in Margit Franz/Heimo Halbrainer/Gabriele Anderl (eds), *Going East. Going South. Österreichisches Exil in Asien und Afrika*, Graz 2013, pp. 165–182, here pp. 171–177.
10. Handwritten Arabic marriage certificate, Yad Vashem Archives, M. 31/12582.
11. See Michael H. Kater, *Different Drummers: Jazz in the Culture of Nazi Germany*, New York 1992, p. 64.
12. See Gerhard Höpp, '"Die Sache ist von immenser Wichtigkeit…". Arabische Studenten in Berlin', manuscript from the estate of Prof. Dr Gerhard Höpp, Centre for Modern Oriental Studies, Berlin, 07.08.005, p. 20.
13. Kater, *Different Drummers*, p. 64.
14. See ibid., p. 42.
15. See Knud Wolffram, *Tanzdielen und Vergnügungspaläste. Berliner Nachtleben in den dreißiger und vierziger Jahren. Von der Friedrichstraße bis Berlin W, von Moka Efti bis zum Delphi*, Berlin 1992, p. 189.
16. *Berliner Herold*, No. 4, 24 January 1932, quoted in ibid., p. 189.
17. See Kater, *Different Drummers*, p. 42 and p. 64.
18. Handwritten marriage certificate, Yad Vashem Archives, M. 31/12582.

## Chapter 13

1. Interviews of September 2016 with Carla Gutman Greenspan and Charles Gutman.
2. See Anna's report of 10 July 1945, Yad Vashem Archives, M. 31/12582.
3. Letter of 21 June 1943 from the Berlin-Charlottenburg registry office to Abdel Aziz Helmy Hammad, Gutman family archive.
4. See David Motadel, *Islam and Nazi Germany's War*, Cambridge, Massachusetts/London 2014, p. 57 f.
5. Dr Helmy's affidavit of 9 February 1953 for submission to the Compensation Board; notarized copy in LABO Berlin, Reg. No. 14 500, fols. C 10–16.
6. Letter of 21 June 1943 from the Berlin-Charlottenburg registry office to Hammad, Gutman family archive.
7. Letter of 5 July 1943 from the Romanian Consulate to Anna, Gutman family archive.

8. Dr Helmy's affidavit of 9 February 1953 for submission to the Compensation Board, notarized copy in LABO Berlin, Reg. No. 14 500, fols. C 10–16.
9. Anna's report of 10 July 1945, Yad Vashem Archives, M. 31/12582.
10. Unpublished research by Sabine Mülder and Dr Karsten Mülder, Berlin.

## Chapter 14

1. See Anna's compensation case file, LABO Berlin, Reg. No. 52 472, fol. C 2.
2. See Anna's report of 10 July 1945, Yad Vashem Archives, M. 31/12582.
3. Ibid.
4. See compensation case file Julie Wehr, LABO Berlin, Reg. No. 72 475, fol. B 12, E 2.
5. See compensation case file Georg Wehr, LABO Berlin, Reg. No. 71 761, fol. E 25.
6. See compensation case file Martin Rudnik, LABO Berlin, Reg. No. 23 973, fol. B 4, B 7, B 17.
7. See ibid., fol. C 8 f.
8. See ibid.
9. Anna's report of 10 July 1945 and Julie Wehr's report of 26 September 1945, Yad Vashem Archives, M. 31/12582.
10. See ibid.
11. Dr Helmy's affidavit of 9 February 1953 for submission to the Compensation Board, notarized copy in LABO Berlin, Reg. No. 14 500, fols. C 10–16, and Anna's own autobiographical account of 1 November 1945, Yad Vashem Archives, M. 31/12582.
12. See Anna's report of 10 July 1945, Yad Vashem Archives, M. 31/12582, Dr Helmy's affidavit of 9 February 1953 for submission to the Compensation Board, notarized copy in LABO Berlin, Reg. No. 14 500, fols. C 10–16.
13. See Anna's compensation case file, LABO Berlin, Reg. No. 52472, fol. B1, B 12f., B 24.
14. See Peter Warnecke, *Laube, Liebe, Hoffnung. Kleingartengeschichte*, Berlin 2001, p. 48 f.
15. See Anna's handwritten autobiographical account of 1 November 1945 and her report of 10 July 1945, Yad Vashem Archives, M. 31/12582.
16. See Anna's handwritten autobiographical account of December 1953, Berlin State Archive, B Rep. 078, No. 0561 ('Unsung Heroes' collection, application Mohd Helmy), fols. 13–16, here p. 15.

17. See ibid.
18. Julie Wehr's report of 26 September 1945, Yad Vashem Archives, M. 31/12582.
19. Anna's report of 10 July 1945, Yad Vashem Archives, M. 31/12582.
20. Ibid.; also Dr Helmy's affidavit of 9 February 1953 for submission to the Compensation Board, notarized copy in LABO Berlin, Reg. No. 14 500, fols. C 10–16.
21. See compensation case file Julie Wehr, LABO Berlin, Reg. No. 72475, fol. C 2.
22. Julie Wehr's report of 26 September 1945, Yad Vashem Archives, M. 31/12582.
23. Anna's report of 10 July 1945, Yad Vashem Archives, M. 31/12582.
24. Dr Helmy's affidavit of 9 February 1953 for submission to the Compensation Board, notarized copy in LABO Berlin, Reg. No. 14 500, fols. C 10–16.

## Chapter 15

1. Helmy's affidavit of 11 May 1954 for submission to the Compensation Board, Berlin State Archive, B Rep. 078, No. 0561 ('Unsung Heroes' collection, application Mohd Helmy), fol. 17.
2. Robert Satloff, *Among the Righteous. Lost Stories from the Holocaust's Long Reach into Arab Lands*, New York 2006, p. 173.
3. Ibid., pp. 141–151.
4. Sonja Hegasy, 'Araber und Nazi-Deutschland: "Kollaborateure und Widersacher"', published online at https://www.qantara.de on 1.12.2010.
5. Satloff, *Among the Righteous*, p. 2.
6. See Helmy's letter of 24 October 1939 to the Iranian legation and his letter of 8 December 1939 to Hitler, both in the Foreign Office Political Archive, R 27262.
7. Helmy's letter of 25 October 1939 to the Foreign Office, Foreign Office Political Archive, R 27262. See also Helmy's letter of 13.13.1939 [sic] to Consul Dr Melches, ibid.: 'Moreover, I am half-German'.
8. Dr Helmy's affidavit of 9 February 1953 for submission to the Compensation Board, notarized copy in LABO Berlin, Reg. No. 14 500, fols. C 10–16.
9. Helmy's letter of 16 December 1959 to the Cairo city authorities (application for new birth certificate), el-Kelish family archive.

10. Letter from Anna Gutman to Henry Gutman, undated, Gutman family archive.
11. Ibid.
12. Letter of 12 August 1947 from Anna Gutman to Henry Gutman, Gutman family archive.

# BIOGRAPHIES

ANNA BOROS (b.22 November 1925 in Arad, Western Romania, on the border with Hungary), came to Berlin at the age of two with her mother Julie. She started school in 1931 and was forced to switch to a Jewish school in 1938. In 1942, she took refuge with Dr Helmy. After 1945, while still in Berlin, she married the Polish Orthodox Jew Chaim Gutman, who had trained as a radio technician in a Displaced Persons Camp. Together, they emigrated to the USA. Chaim became known as Hans and ultimately Henry, while Anna worked as a nanny for an American doctor before having three children of her own. She lived in New York up to her death in 1986, and sent her children to Jewish schools. She visited her rescuer Dr Helmy twice in Berlin. On one of her visits, she took her daughter Carla with her and proudly introduced them to each other.

DR HELMUT DENNIG (b.13 July 1895), a member of the NSDAP (Nazi Party), became chief physician of the Internal Medicine Department I at Moabit hospital, and hence Dr Helmy's supervisor, in 1934. After vilifying Helmy as an 'Oriental' and forcing him out of the hospital in 1937, Dennig worked from 1939 to the end of the war as a consultant internist with the *Wehrmacht*. After the end of the war, he became head of the Internal Medicine Department of Stuttgart's Karl-Olga Hospital. At the Nuremberg Doctors' Trial, he testified in favour of a former junior doctor at Moabit, Hermann Becker-Freyseng, who was accused of conducting human experiments at Dachau. In 1947, he became a state physician of the German Red Cross and, in 1956, a member of the Drug Commission of the German Medical Association.

EMMY ANNA AUGUSTE ERNST (b.19 March 1916 in Berlin) was working as a medical nurse when she met Dr Helmy in Berlin. The couple became engaged in 1939, but were unable to obtain official approval for their marriage on grounds of 'race'. Emmy assisted Helmy with his medical work as well as his clandestine rescue activities. They were finally able to marry after the end of the war in June 1945. They subsequently paid several visits to Helmy's family in Egypt, with whom Emmy kept in close contact even after Helmy's death in 1982 and, indeed, until her own death in Berlin in 1998. Although she could only speak broken Arabic, Emmy sometimes joked to Helmy's young nephews in Egypt that she had been Egyptian longer than them, having obtained an Egyptian passport through her marriage in 1945.

DR KAMAL EL-DIN GALAL (b.1903) came to Berlin in 1922 together with Helmy, and studied journalism at the Technical University in Charlottenburg. After gaining a doctorate on the 'Origin and Development of the Daily Press in Egypt' in 1939, he worked as a correspondent for the Egyptian newspapers *Al-Balagh* and *Al-Ahram*. As an ardent nationalist and anti-colonialist, he was also involved in the Egyptian Students' Association and was General Secretary of the Islamic Central Institute from 1942. His closeness to the Nazi regime and to the Grand Mufti of Jerusalem in particular enabled Galal to play an important role in Helmy's secret rescue campaigns. He continued to live in West Germany long after the war, where he served as Egypt's press attaché.

ABDEL AZIZ HELMY HAMMAD (b.6 May 1906 in Fakous, Egypt) came to Berlin in 1924 to study, but subsequently became more immersed in the artistic than the academic world. His family was prominent on the political stage in Egypt, his father being mayor of the town of Fakous. The young Hammad was accompanied to Berlin by his new bride, Fatma, chosen by his father, but the relationship broke up, and Fatma returned to Egypt with their small child. Hammad turned to jazz, his true passion, and became a successful manager of the Carlton Bar near the Kurfürstendamm. Perhaps he and Helmy had already crossed paths at one of Berlin's Arab student clubs, but they got to know each other during the months of their internment in 1939 by the Gestapo. Hammad played an important role in Helmy's network of Muslim friends who helped him secretly with his rescue activities. What became of him after the war is not known.

DR MOHAMED 'MOHD' HELMY (b.25 July 1901 in Khartoum, then British Egypt, as Mohamed Helmy Abu el-Ainin Said Ahmed) was the fourth of five children born to the Egyptian army major Abu el-Ainin Said Ahmed and his wife, Amina Reda Hassan el-Komi. During the Nazi period, Helmy is reputed to have briefly claimed that his mother was German, but old family chronicles and Helmy's own Arabic correspondence with Cairo authorities in 1959 prove this to be merely a story concocted in order to throw the Nazis off the scent, and he clarified in 1959 that his mother was 'Egyptian and a Muslim'. He began his degree in medicine at Berlin's Friedrich-Wilhelm University in 1922 and became a junior doctor at Moabit hospital in 1930, then a senior consultant in 1933. On the advice of his German partner, Helmy made a point of using his nickname Mohd, which he shortened further to Mod after the war for practical reasons, since many Germans had difficulties with the name Mohamed. In 1937, he was driven out of the clinic by the Nazis, and continued to practise privately, first at his home, Krefelder Straße 7, then at a surgery in Charlottenburg. This was where he executed the plan that saved the life of the Jewish girl Anna Boros. After liberation in 1945, he married his long-time partner, Emmy, and continued to practise as a doctor in Berlin for many decades. He remained in correspondence with Anna for the rest of his life. He died in Berlin in 1982.

GRAND MUFTI MOHAMED AMIN AL-HUSSEINI (b.1897 in Jerusalem) served as Hitler's chief propagandist in the Muslim world. The honorific 'mufti' means 'interpreter of the law' and refers to a Muslim scholar to whom religious questions can be addressed. An official state mufti is known as a Grand Mufti, a role that still exists to this day in Saudi Arabia and Egypt. Amin al-Husseini was the official state mufti in Palestine at the time of the British mandate rule. This was a powerful position, as Husseini faced no competition from a parallel Muslim government: he was effectively the sole representative of the Muslim population. During the Second World War, he supported the Nazis, and fled to Berlin in 1941 to escape the British. His staff of around sixty Arab propagandists and recruiters for the Nazis—paid for by the NS regime—operated under the name of 'Mufti office' and was accountable to the Reich Main Security Office. The claim that the Mufti persuaded Hitler to instigate the Holocaust, as Israel's Prime Minister Benjamin

Netanyahu once asserted, is a myth, however: the destruction programme was already under way when the Mufti came to Berlin. Until his death in Beirut in 1974, Husseini continued to serve as a figurehead for militant Palestinian groups under the leadership of Yasser Arafat.

RIAD AHMED MOHAMED (b.15 September 1899 in Cairo) represented a moderate, comparatively pro-British, approach based on international understanding rather than the struggle for liberation. He led various associations and groups at different times, such as the Islamic Community and the German Muslim Society. In 1939, with the support of a few German converts to Islam, he revived the Islam Institute in Berlin as an intellectual authority. When the Nazis imprisoned him along with other Egyptians following the outbreak of war in autumn 1939, the leadership of the Institute was taken over by the fiercely anti-British Arab nationalist Kamal el-Din Galal. What became of him after the war is unknown.

DR HUGO 'HAMID' MARCUS (b.6 July 1880 in Posen, now Poznan, Poland), the son of a Jewish family of industrialists, was a Berlin intellectual of the Weimar period. Around the turn of the century, Marcus—as a writer of bestselling esoteric and pacifist books and a Doctor of Philosophy—had been one of the most eccentric figures of the Berlin literary scene. In the early 1920s, he converted to Islam and took the name Hamid. From 1923 to 1938, he was the business manager of the Berlin mosque. He edited the journal *Moslemische Revue*, translated the Quran into German, and was even President of the German Muslim Society from 1930 to 1935, despite remaining a member of the Jewish community. In 1938, he escaped with Muslim assistance and went into exile in Switzerland, where he survived the war. He continued to write for a long time under the pseudonym Hans Alienus for *Der Kreis*, an internationally acclaimed gay magazine.

ANNA'S GRANDMOTHER CECILIE RUDNIK, née Klein (b.27 October 1875 in Hódmeszövásárhely, Hungary), came to Berlin at the age of seventeen in order to help her brother, who was already running a thriving fruit and vegetable business. She learned quickly and became a successful saleswoman, travelling back and forth between Hungary and Berlin. After the unexpected death in 1912 of her first husband, Moritz Schwarz, with whom she had one daughter, Julie, she continued to trade successfully in her own right. In 1914, she married the businessman Moise Rudnik, with whom she had a son, Martin. After liberation in 1945, Cecilie's relationship with her daughter Julie and her granddaughter Anna was never really restored; the years of hiding had also been years of conflict. Instead, Cecilie went to Israel with her son Martin. Disappointed by the country's major economic problems, however, she returned after a few years to Berlin, where she died in 1953.

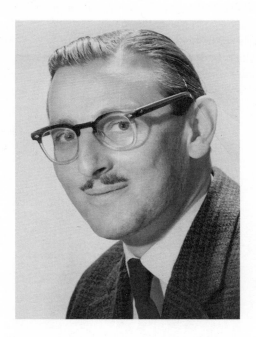

ANNA'S UNCLE MARTIN RUDNIK (b.7 March 1918 in Berlin), Cecilie's son from her second marriage and Julie's half-brother, had begun an apprenticeship as a dental assistant when the Nazis forced him to quit. From 1940 onwards, he was conscripted into forced labour at a sheet metal processing plant in Weißensee. In 1942, he fled to avoid deportation, hiding out at the homes of various Berlin friends—notably the dressmaker

Hildegard Ullbrich from Wilmersdorf, whom he had known since 1941 through a mutual Jewish friend, Ursula Redlich. He became engaged to another of his helpers, Vera Köhler, but after the war he eventually married the Viennese nightclub dancer Luana, an African circus artist's daughter, in Berlin. The couple first went to Israel, where Luana got a job as a dancer in Haifa. Martin was unable to find work, however, and struggled to support his by now seventy-year-old mother, Cecilie, who had accompanied them there. Disheartened, they returned to Berlin. It was only after Cecilie's death in 1953 that Martin and Luana were able to start a successful new life in New York.

ANNA'S STEPGRANDFATHER MOISE 'MAX' RUDNIK (b.22 October 1877 in Iasi, Romania) founded the greengrocery M. Rudnik GmbH, Neue Friedrichstraße 77, in Berlin in 1929, but contracted stomach cancer in 1930, after which he became dependent on care. Anna's mother, Julie, looked after him while simultaneously running the business with Anna's grandmother Cecilie. He died in 1939 at the Jewish hospital and was buried in Weißensee.

FRIEDA SZTURMANN (b.12 June 1897) was a mother and homeworker who lived in Staaken, near Spandau. As a long-time patient of Dr Helmy, she was someone he knew well and could turn to when, in March 1942, he had to find a discreet hiding place for a Jewish girl at short notice. For many years, Frieda Szturmann risked her life hiding first Cecile Rudnik and later, for a brief period, Anna Boros. Like Helmy, Frieda Szturmann was awarded the posthumous honour of 'Righteous Among the Nations' by the Yad Vashem Holocaust Memorial Center in 2013. The certificate was presented to her grandson Dieter by the Israeli ambassador to Berlin. After the war, she remained Dr Helmy's patient for many years, and lived in Staaken with her retired husband and son until her death in 1966.

ANNA'S MOTHER JULIANNA 'JULIE' WEHR, née Schwarz (b.14 September 1902 in Oroshaza, Hungary), grew up in Hungary. After divorcing her first husband, the Jewish factory owner Ladislaus Boros from Arad, in 1927, she moved with her young daughter Anna to Berlin, where she played an important role in the greengrocery business run by her mother. In 1929, she married the Berliner Georg Wehr, who was not a Jew according to the logic of Nazi laws, even though he had converted to her faith. In 1942, Julie was conscripted into forced labour, but her marriage with a non-Jew protected her from a worse fate. In 1946, she turned her back on Germany for good and went out to join her daughter in the USA. She worked as a chef in Detroit, earning fifty dollars a week, but soon found the work too hard and gave it up. Her American dream of opening a Hungarian restaurant together with her daughter, to whom she once confided the idea, remained unfulfilled.

ANNA'S STEPFATHER GEORG WEHR (b.22 August 1904 in Thorn, now Torun, Poland) worked as a delicatessen salesman in Berlin and did not convert to Judaism until 1929, after marrying the greengrocer's daughter Julie Wehr. In October 1943, it was ruled that men 'of German blood' who were married to Jews should be sent likewise to labour camps run by the engineering enterprise Organisation Todt, and Wehr was duly dispatched to Forced Labour Camp 3 in Jena on 9 November 1944. 'Everyone was afraid of getting shot', he later recalled. During the five months he spent there, he lost almost sixty pounds. After liberation, he made his way back to Berlin on foot. In 1946, reunited with Julie, he emigrated to the USA.

# TIMELINE

## Nazi Islam Policy

The German Reich had sought to curry favour with Muslims long before 1933. At a time when the Muslim world was almost completely under British, French, or Soviet rule, the strategy of 'revolutionizing the Muslim nations' on the territory of Germany's opponents was already well established. 'Kaiser Wilhelm II has converted to Islam', reads a German propaganda pamphlet of 1915 designed to win Arab support for the Germans in the war. The text continues: 'He has renamed himself Hadji Wilhelm Mohamed and has already undertaken a secret pilgrimage to Mecca. More and more Germans are following his example and becoming Mohammedans.' The Nazis took these propaganda campaigns to extremes, however, as demonstrated by the historian David Motadel, who has written what is probably the best book on this subject. In the Balkans, in Central Asia, and in North Africa—in short, in all the strategically relevant fringes of Europe—they encountered Muslim populations, with whom they hoped to forge an alliance against their common enemies, notably the British and Jews.

1 July 1936: At a Foreign Office meeting, representatives from key ministries and the racial policy department of the NSDAP rule that Turkish, Persian, and Arab Muslims are not 'aliens' within the meaning of the Nuremberg race laws. In medieval Spain, laws on 'blood purity' had applied to Jews and Muslims alike.

1939: NS propaganda minister Joseph Goebbels issues detailed instructions to the German press requiring it to refrain in future from all contemptuous references to 'Mussulmen'.

November 1939: Germany's only mosque, built in Berlin-Wilmersdorf in 1925, loses its leader when the outbreak of war causes the imam Muhammad Abdullah, a scholar with a doctorate in chemistry from Friedrich-Wilhelm University, to return to his home country of India.

11 February 1941: German troops land on the beaches of Tripoli in Libya and begin to push towards Cairo, as Hitler comes to Italy's aid. Since the end of 1940, Mussolini's forces have been forced onto the defensive in the fight against Britain in North Africa.

April 1941: The NS troops recruit Muslim Albanians to their Balkan campaign. Thereafter, Muslims are also enlisted from among Soviet prisoners of war, who are treated abominably by the Germans.

May 1941: In Iraq, meanwhile, the nationalist leader Rashid Ali al-Gailani has seized power in a military coup. His campaign against the former colonial power of Britain is supported by German fighter planes, but the German *Sonderkommando Junck* is quickly defeated. Before going into exile in Berlin, Gailani manages to instigate a pogrom—the *Farhud*—against Baghdad's Jews.

6 November 1941: The Grand Mufti of Jerusalem, Amin al-Husseini, flees to Berlin to escape the British. From now on, as a guest of honour of the SS, he is enlisted in the Nazi propaganda campaign, appearing regularly on the international radio station Radio Berlin. His addresses are broadcast in Arabic, Persian, and Turkish.

18 November 1941: The former German envoy to Cairo and now ambassador to Madrid, Eberhard von Stohrer, issues a memorandum recommending 'an extensive German Islam programme' and calling for the formation of a 'committee of Islam experts under the direction of the Foreign Office'.

13 January 1942: The *Wehrmacht* forms the 'Turkestan legion' and the 'Caucasian-Mohammedan legion', consisting almost exclusively of Muslims. Azerbaijanis, Crimean and Volga Tatars, North Caucasians, Bashkirs, Uzbeks, and others are soon given the opportunity to serve in other 'eastern legions'.

20 July 1942: The staff of Hitler's general in Africa, Erwin Rommel, authorizes a special extermination unit under the command of SS senior commander Walther Rauff to kill all Jews resident in Palestine in the event of the country's defeat.

23 August 1942: Beginning of the five-month battle of Stalingrad, whose huge losses for the German army bring about a change in the course of the war.

September 1942: German troops cross the border into Egypt. At the same time, Radio Berlin's Arabic programme for the North African population broadcasts messages such as 'Kill the Jews before they kill you', and 'Once again, we thank God that Egypt is being cleansed of these poisonous reptiles'.

11 October 1942: At the feast of Eid (breaking of the fast), the Grand Mufti delivers a belligerent speech to five hundred guests at the Wilmersdorf mosque.

November 1942: After months of standstill, the German troops are repelled by the British in the Egyptian town of El-Alamein, ninety miles from Cairo.

18 December 1942: The Islamic Central Institute is opened in Berlin with a ceremonial address by the Grand Mufti.

10 February 1943: SS chief Himmler gives permission for the creation of a Waffen-SS unit consisting of Muslims from the Balkans. The Bosnian '13th Waffen Mountain Division of the SS Handschar' is duly formed, named after the Arabic word for a scimitar.

1–11 April 1943: The Grand Mufti undertakes a trip across the Balkans attempting to mobilize Muslims for the Waffen-SS.

13 May 1943: The last remaining German troops in North Africa concede victory to the British in Tunis.

1 March 1944: The Grand Mufti broadcasts a speech on Radio Berlin: 'Kill the Jews wherever you find them. This pleases God, history, and religion.' Turkmenian Waffen-SS soldiers begin to attend the Wilmersdorf mosque.

21 April 1944: The *Wehrmacht* opens its own imam school in Guben where field imams are trained to stir up Muslim recruits.

June 1944: The University of Göttingen launches a programme of 'mullah courses' to provide prospective field imams with ideological instruction.

16 November 1944: An SS mullah school is founded in Dresden at the behest of SS chief Himmler.

April 1945: In the final phase of the battle for Berlin, German troops use the minaret of the Wilmersdorf mosque as an artillery command post, bringing the mosque directly into the firing line. Twelve German soldiers are later found dead in the garden and are buried there in a temporary mass grave.

# PICTURE CREDITS

# INDEX

Note: Figures are indicated by an italic "f", respectively, following the page number.

For the benefit of digital users, indexed terms that span two pages (e.g., 52–53) may, on occasion, appear on only one of those pages.